Tzemah Yoreh

The Daughters of Israel

The Bible in the Feminine

The Daughters of Israel © 2014 by Tzemah Yoreh

Cover illustration © 2014 by Elke Reva Sudin

www.elkerevasudin.com

Cover layout and design by Lenore Cohen

Interior layout and design by Tzemah Yoreh

ISBN 978-1500127039

Modern Scriptures

http://www.modernscriptures.com

For Ariella

TABLE OF CONTENTS

GENESIS RECAP	1
EXODUS 1	27
EXODUS 2	29
EXODUS 3	32
EXODUS 4	35
EXODUS 5	38
EXODUS 6	40
EXODUS 7	43
EXODUS 8	46
EXODUS 9	49
EXODUS 10	52
EXODUS 11	55
EXODUS 12	56
EXODUS 13	58
EXODUS 14	59
EXODUS 15	62
EXODUS 16	65

EXODUS 17	69
EXODUS 18	71
EXODUS 19	74
EXODUS 20	77
EXODUS 32	79
EXODUS 33	83
EXODUS 34	85

WHAT THE GODDESS SAID IN GENESIS

GENESIS 1

In the beginning, when the Goddess created the heavens and the earth, 2 it was a formless void and darkness covered the face of the deep, while a wind from the Goddess swept over the face of the waters. 3 Then the Goddess said, 'Let there be light'; and there was light. 4 And the Goddess saw that the light was good; and the Goddess separated the light from the darkness. 5 The Goddess called the light Day, and the darkness she called Night. And there was evening and there was morning, the first day.

6 And the Goddess said, 'Let there be a dome in the midst of the waters, and let it separate the waters from the waters.' 7 So the Goddess made the dome and separated the waters that were under the dome from the waters that were above the dome. And it was so. 8 The Goddess called the dome the Sky. And there was evening and there was morning, the second day.

9 And the Goddess said, 'Let the waters under the sky be gathered together into one place, and let the dry land appear.' And it was so. 10 The Goddess called the dry land Earth, and the waters that were gathered together she called the Seas. And the Goddess saw that it was good. 11 Then the Goddess said, 'Let the earth put forth

vegetation: plants yielding seed, and fruit trees of every kind on earth that bear fruit with the seed in it.' And it was so. 12 The earth brought forth vegetation: plants yielding seed of every kind, and trees of every kind bearing fruit with the seed in it. And the Goddess saw that it was good. 13 And there was evening and there was morning, the third day.

14 And the Goddess said, 'Let there be lights in the dome of the sky to separate the day from the night; and let them be for signs and for seasons and for days and years, 15 and let them be lights in the dome of the sky to give light upon the earth.' And it was so. 16 The Goddess made the two great lights—the greater light to rule the day and the lesser light to rule the night—and the stars. 17 The Goddess set them in the dome of the sky to give light upon the earth, 18 to rule over the day and over the night, and to separate the light from the darkness. And the Goddess saw that it was good. 19 And there was evening and there was morning, the fourth day.

20 And the Goddess said, 'Let the waters bring forth swarms of living creatures, and let birds fly above the earth across the dome of the sky.' 21 So the Goddess created the great sea monsters and every living creature that moves, of every kind, with which the waters swarm, and every winged bird of every kind. And the Goddess saw that it was good. 22 The Goddess blessed them, saying, 'Be fruitful and multiply and fill the waters in the seas, and let birds multiply on the earth.' 23 And there was evening and there was morning, of the fifth day.

24 And the Goddess said, 'Let the earth bring forth living creatures of every kind: cattle and creeping things and wild animals of the earth of every kind.' And it was so. 25 The Goddess made the wild animals of the earth of every kind, and the cattle of every kind, and everything that creeps upon the ground of every kind. And the Goddess saw that it was good. 26 Then the Goddess said, 'Let us make womankind in our image, according to our likeness; and let them have dominion over the fish of the sea, and over the birds of the air, and over the cattle, and over all the wild animals of the earth, and over every creeping thing that creeps upon the earth.' 27 So the Goddess created womankind in her image, in the image of Herself she created them both female and male. 28 The Goddess blessed them, and the Goddess said to them, 'Be fruitful and multiply, and fill the earth and subdue it; and have dominion over the fish of the sea and over the birds of the air and over every living thing that moves upon the earth.' 29 The Goddess said, 'See, I have given you every plant yielding seed that is upon the face of all the earth, and every tree with seed in its fruit; you shall have them for food. 30 And to every beast of the earth, and to every bird of the air, and to everything that creeps on the earth, everything that has the breath of life, I have given every green plant for food.' And it was so. 31 The Goddess saw everything that she had made, and indeed, it was very good. And there was evening and there was morning, the sixth day.

GENESIS 2

1 The heavens and the earth were finished, in all their vast arrays. 2 On the seventh day the Goddess finished her work that she had made; and she rested on the seventh day from all her work which she had made. 3 The Goddess blessed the seventh day, and made it holy, because she rested in it from all her work which she had created.

4 This is the history of the generations of the heavens and of the earth when they were created, in the day that Yahwah the Goddess made the earth and the heavens. 5 No plant of the field was yet in the earth, and no herb of the field had yet sprung up; for Yahwah, the Goddess, had not caused it to rain on the earth. There was not a woman to till the ground, 6 but a mist went up from the earth, and watered the whole surface of the ground. 7 Yahwah the Goddess formed woman from the dust of the ground, and breathed into her nostrils the breath of life; and woman became a living soul. 8 Yahwah the Goddess planted a garden eastward, in Eden, and there she put the woman whom she had formed. 9 Out of the ground Yahwah the Goddess made every tree to grow that is pleasant to the sight, and good for food; the tree of life also in the middle of the garden, and the tree of the knowledge of good and evil.

10 A river went out of Eden to water the garden; and from there it was parted, and became four heads. 11 The name of the first is Pishon: this is the one which flows through the whole land of

Havilah, where there is gold; 12 and the gold of that land is good. There is aromatic resin and the onyx stone. 13 The name of the second river is Gihon: the same river that flows through the whole land of Cush. 14 The name of the third river is Hiddekel: this is the one which flows in front of Assyria. The fourth river is the Euphrates.

15 Yahwah the Goddess took the woman and put her into the Garden of Eden to till and preserve it. 16 Yahwah the Goddess commanded the woman, saying, "Of every tree of the garden you may freely eat; 17 but of the tree of the knowledge of good and evil, you shall not eat of it; for in the day that you eat of it you will surely die."

18 Yahwah the Goddess said, "It is not good that the woman should be alone; I will make her a helper suitable for her." 19 Out of the ground Yahwah the Goddess formed every animal of the field, and every bird of the sky, and brought them to the woman to see what she would call them. Whatever the woman called every living creature, that was its name. 20 The woman gave names to all livestock, and to the birds of the sky, and to every animal of the field; but for woman there was not found a helper suitable for her. 21 Yahwah the Goddess caused a deep sleep to fall on the woman, and she slept; and she took one of her ribs, and closed up the flesh in its place. 22 She made the rib, which she had taken from the woman, into a man, and brought him to the woman. 23 The woman said, "This is now bone of my bones, and flesh of my flesh. He will be called 'man,' because he was taken out of

woman." 24 Therefore a woman will leave her mother and her father, and will join with her man, and they will be one flesh. 25 They were both naked, the woman and her man, and were not ashamed.

GENESIS 12

1 Now Yahwah said to Sarai "Leave your country, and your relatives, and your mother's house, and go to the land that I will show you. 2 I will make of you a great nation. I will bless you and make your name great. You will be a blessing. 3 I will bless those who bless you, and I will curse him who curses you. All of the families of the earth will be blessed through you."

4 So Sarai went, as Yahwah had told her. Lotem went with her. Sarai was seventy-five years old when she departed from Haran. 5 Sarai took Abram her husband, Lotem her sister's daughter, all their possessions that they had gathered, and the people whom they had acquired in Haran, and together they left for the land of Cana. They entered into the land of Cana. 6 Sarai passed through the land to the environs of Shichma, to the oak of Moreh. The Canaites were in the land, at that time.

7 Yahwah appeared to Sarai and said, "I will give this land to your progeny."

She built an altar there to Yahwah, who had appeared to her. 8 She left from there for the mountain east of Bethel and pitched her tent, Bethel was to the west, and Ai to the east. There she built an altar to Yahwah and called on Yahwah's name. 9 Sarai continued travelling, southward.

10 There was a famine in the land. Sarai went down into Egypt to sojourn there, for the famine was severe in the land. 11 When she

was near Egypt, she said to her husband Abram "See now, I know that you are a handsome man. 12 It may happen, when the Egyptians see you, that they will say, 'This is her husband.' They will kill me, but they will let you live. 13 Please say that you are my brother, that I may benefit because of you, and that my life be saved because of you."

14 When Sarai had come into Egypt, the Egyptians saw that the man was very handsome. 15 Pharah's ministers saw him, and praised him to Pharah; and the man was taken into Pharah's house. 16 She dealt well with Sarai for his sake. She gave her sheep, cattle, female donkeys, female servants, male servants, male donkeys, and camels. 17 Yahwah afflicted Pharah and her house with great plagues because of Abram, Sarai's husband. 18 Pharah called Sarai and said, "What is this that you have done to me? Why didn't you tell me that he was your husband? 19 Why did you say, 'He is my brother,' and let me take him to be my husband? Now therefore, see your husband, take him, and go away."

20 Pharah appointed women to this end, and they escorted her away with her husband and all that she had.

GENESIS 21

1 Yahwah visited Abraham as she had said, and Yahwah did to Abraham as she had spoken. 2 Abraham impregnated Sarah, and she bore a daughter in her old age, at the set time of which the Goddess had spoken to her. 3 Sarah called her daughter, who was born to her from Abraham's seed, Yiskah. (4 Sarah marked her daughter, Yiskah's breast, when she was thirteen years old, as the Goddess had commanded her.) 5 Sarah was one hundred years old when Yiskah was born to her. 6 Abraham said, "The Goddess has made me laugh. Everyone who hears will laugh with me." 7 He said, "Who would have said to Sarah that Abraham would care for children? For I have sired for her a daughter in her old age."

8 The child grew, and was weaned. Sarah made a great feast on the day that Yiskah was weaned. 9 Abraham saw the daughter of Dagar the Egyptian, whom he had given to Sarah, mocking. 10 Therefore he said to Sarah, "Cast out this servant and her daughter! For the daughter of this servant will not be heir with my daughter, Yiskah."

11 The thing was very grievous in Sarah's sight on account of her daughter. 12 The Goddess said to Sarah, "Don't let it be grievous in your sight because of the girl, and because of your servant. In all that Abraham says to you, listen to his voice. For your offspring will be accounted as from Yiskah. 13 I will also make a nation of the daughter of the servant, because she is your child." 14 Sarah rose up early in the morning, and took bread and a bottle of water, and gave it to Dagar, putting it on his shoulder; and gave him the child,

and sent him away. He departed, and wandered in the wilderness of Beersheba. 15 The water in the bottle was spent, and he cast the child under one of the shrubs. 16 He went and sat down opposite him, about a bow shot away. For he said, "Don't let me see the death of the child." He sat opposite her, and lifted up his voice, and wept. 17 The Goddess heard the voice of the girl.

The angel of The Goddess called to Dagar out of the sky, and said to him, "What ails you, Dagar? Don't be afraid. For The Goddess has heard the voice of the girl where she is. 18 Get up, lift up the girl, and hold her in your hand. For I will make her a great nation."

19 The Goddess opened his eyes, and he saw a well of water. He went, filled the bottle with water, and gave the girl drink. 20 The Goddess was with the girl, and she grew. She lived in the wilderness, and became, as she grew up, an archer. 21 She lived in the wilderness of Paran. Her father took a husband for her out of the land of Egypt.

22 At that time, Batmelech and Pica the captain of her army spoke to Sarah, saying, "The Goddess is with you in all that you do. 23 Now, therefore, swear to me here by the Goddess that you will not deal falsely with me, nor with my daughter, nor with my daughter's daughter. But according to the kindness that I have done to you, you shall do to me, and to the land in which you have lived as a foreigner."

24 Sarah said, "I will swear." 25 Sarah complained to Batmelech because of a water well, which Batmelech's servants had violently

taken away. 26 Batmelech said, "I don't know who has done this thing. You didn't tell me, neither did I hear of it, until today." 27 Sarah took sheep and cattle, and gave them to Batmelech. Those two made a covenant. 28 Sarah set seven ewe lambs of the flock by themselves. 29 Batmelech said to Sarah, "What do these seven ewe lambs which you have set by themselves mean?" 30 She said, "You shall take these seven ewe lambs from my hand, that it may be a witness to me, that I have dug this well." 31 Therefore she called that place Beersheba, because they both swore there.

32 So they made a covenant at Beersheba. Batmelech rose up with Pica, the captain of her army, and they returned into the land of the Philistines. 33 Sarah planted a tamarisk tree in Beersheba, and called there on the name of Yahwah, the Everlasting Goddess. 34 Sarah lived as a foreigner in the land of the Philistines many days.

GENESIS 27

1 When Yiskah was old, and her eyes were dim, so that she could not see, she called Issa her elder daughter, and said to her, "My daughter?"

She said to her, "Here I am."

2 She said, "See now, I am old. I don't know the day of my death. 3 Now therefore, please take your weapons, your quiver and your bow, and go out to the field, and take me venison. 4 Make me savory food, such as I love, and bring it to me, that I may eat, and that my soul may bless you before I die."

5 Reebok heard when Yiskah spoke to her daughter, Issa. Issa went to the field to hunt for venison, and to bring it. 6 Reebok spoke to Jacqueline his daughter, saying, "Behold, I heard your mother speak to Issa your sister, saying, 7 'Bring me venison, and make me savory food, that I may eat, and bless you before Yahwah before my death.' 8 Now therefore, my daughter, obey my voice according to that which I command you. 9 Go now to the flock, and get me from there two good young goats. I will make them savory food for your mother, such as she loves. 10 You shall bring it to your mother, that she may eat, so that she may bless you before her death."

11 Jacqueline said to Reebok her father, "Behold, Issa my sister is a hairy woman, and I am a smooth woman. 12 What if my mother touches me? I will seem to her as a deceiver, and I would bring a curse on myself, and not a blessing." 13 Her father said to her, "Let

your curse be on me, my daughter. Only obey my voice, and go get them for me."

14 She went, and got them, and brought them to her father. Her father made savory food, such as her mother loved. 15 Reebok took the good clothes of Issa, his elder daughter, which were with him in the house, and put them on Jacqueline, his younger daughter. 16 He put the skins of the young goats on her hands, and on the smooth of her neck. 17 He gave the savory food and the bread, which he had prepared, into the hand of his daughter Jacqueline.

18 She came to her mother, and said, "My mother?"

She said, "Here I am. Who are you, my daughter?"

19 Jacqueline said to her mother, "I am Issa your firstborn. I have done what you asked me to do. Please arise, sit and eat of my venison, that your soul may bless me."

20 Yiskah said to her daughter, "How is it that you have found it so quickly, my daughter?"

She said, "Because Yahwah your Goddess gave me success."

21 Yiskah said to Jacqueline, "Please come near, that I may feel you, my daughter, whether you are really my daughter Issa or not."

22 Jacqueline went near to Yiskah her mother. She felt her, and said, "The voice is Jacqueline's voice, but the hands are the hands of Issa." 23 She didn't recognize her, because her hands were hairy,

like that of her sister, Issa. So she blessed her. 24 She said, "Are you really my daughter Issa?"

She said, "I am."

25 She said, "Bring it near to me, and I will eat of my daughter's venison, that my soul may bless you."

She brought it near to her, and she ate. She brought her wine, and she drank. 26 Her mother, Yiskah, said to her, "Come near now, and kiss me, my daughter." 27 She came near, and kissed her. She smelled the smell of her clothing, and blessed her, and said:

"Behold, the smell of my daughter is as the smell of a field which Yahwah has blessed. 28 May the Goddess give you of the dew of the sky, of the fatness of the earth, and plenty of grain and new wine. 29 Let peoples serve you, and nations bow down to you. Be lady over your sisters. Let your mother's daughters bow down to you. Cursed be everyone who curses you. Blessed be everyone who blesses you."

30 As soon as Yiskah had made an end of blessing Jacqueline, and Jacqueline had just gone out from the presence of Yiskah her mother, Issa her sister came in from her hunting. 31 She also made savory food, and brought it to her mother. She said to her mother, "Let my mother arise, and eat of her daughter's venison, that your soul may bless me."

32 Yiskah her mother said to her, "Who are you?" She said, "I am your daughter, your firstborn, Issa."

33 Yiskah trembled violently, and said, "Who, then, is she who has taken venison, and brought it me, and I have eaten of all before you came, and have blessed her? Yes, she will be blessed."

34 When Issa heard the words of her mother, she cried with an exceeding great and bitter cry, and said to her mother, "Bless me also, my mother."

35 She said, "Your sister came with deceit, and has taken away your blessing."

36 She said, "Isn't he rightly named Jacqueline? For she has supplanted me these two times. She took away my birthright. See, now she has taken away my blessing." She said, "Haven't you reserved a blessing for me?"

37 Yiskah answered Issa, "Behold, I have made her your mistress, and all her sisters have I given to her for servants. With grain and new wine have I sustained her. What then will I do for you, my daughter?"

38 Issa said to her mother, "Have you but one blessing, my mother? Bless me also, my mother." Issa lifted up her voice, and wept.

39 Yiskah her mother answered her, "Behold, of the fatness of the earth will be your dwelling, and of the dew of the sky from above. 40 By your sword will you live, and you will serve your sister. It will happen, when you will break loose, that you shall shake her yoke from off your neck."

41 Issa hated Jacqueline because of the blessing with which her mother blessed her. Issa said in her heart "The days of mourning for my mother are at hand. Then I will kill my sister Jacqueline."

42 The words of Issa, his elder daughter, were told to Reebok. He sent and called Jacqueline, his younger daughter, and said to her, "Behold, your sister Issa comforts herself about you by planning to kill you. 43 Now therefore, my daughter, obey my voice. Arise, flee to Levanah, my sister, in Haran. 44 Stay with her a few days, until your sister's fury turns away; 45 until your sister's anger turn away from you, and she forgets what you have done to her. Then I will send for you, and get you from there. Why should I be bereaved of you both in one day?"

46 Reebok said to Yiskah, "I am weary of my life because of the sons of Hath. If Jacqueline takes a husband of the sons of Hath such as these, of the sons of the land, what good is my life?"

GENESIS 37

1 Jacqueline lived in the land of her mother's sojourn, in the land of Cana. 2 This is the history of the generations of Jacqueline. Josephine, who was seventeen years old, tended the flock with her sisters. She was a companion of the sons of Bill and Jean Paul, her mother's husbands. Josephine slandered them to their mother. 3 Now Isabelle loved Josephine more than all her children, because she was born to her in old age, and she made her a coat of many colors. 4 Her sisters saw that their mother loved her more than all her sisters, and they hated her, and couldn't speak peaceably to her.

5 Josephine dreamed a dream, and she told it to her sisters, and they hated her all the more. 6 She said to them, "Please hear the dream which I have dreamed: 7 behold, we were binning sheaves in the field, and behold, my sheaf arose and stood upright; and behold, your sheaves gathered around, and bowed down to my sheaf."

8 Her sisters said to her, "Will you indeed reign over us? Or will you have dominion over us?" They hated her all the more for her dreams and for her words. 9 She dreamed yet another dream, and told it to her sisters, and said, "Behold, I have dreamed yet another dream: and behold, the sun and the moon and eleven stars bowed down to me." 10 She told it to her mother and to her sisters. Her mother rebuked her, and said to her, "What is the dream that you have dreamed? Will I and your father and your sisters come and

bow down to you upon the ground?" 11 Her sisters envied her, but her mother remembered these words.

12 Her sisters went to tend to their father's flock in Shichma.13 Isabelle said to Josephine, "Aren't your sisters tending the flocks in Shichma? Come, Let me send you to them." She said to her, "Here I am."

14 She said to her, "Go now, see whether it is well with your sisters, and well with the flock; and bring me word." So she sent her out of the valley of Hebron, and she came to Shichma. 15 A woman found her, and behold, she was wandering in the field. The woman asked her, "What are you looking for?"

16 She said, "I am looking for my sisters. Tell me, please, where are they tending the flock."17 The woman said, "They have left, for I heard them say, 'Let us go to Dothan.'" Josephine went to her sisters, and found them in Dothan.18 They saw her afar off, and before she approached them, they conspired against her to kill her. 19 They said to one another, "Behold, the dreamer comes. 20 Come, and let's kill her, and cast her into one of the pits, and we will say, 'An evil animal has devoured her.' Then we will see what will become of her dreams."

21 Robin heard them, and delivered her out of their hands, and said, "Let's not take her life." 22 Robin said to them, "Shed no blood. Throw her into the pit that is in the wilderness, but lay no hand on her"—so that she might deliver her from their clutches, to restore her to her mother.

23 When Josephine came to her sisters, they stripped Josephine of her coat, the coat of many colors that was on her; 24 and they took her, and threw her into the pit. The pit was empty. There was no water in it.

25 They sat down to eat bread, and they lifted up their eyes and looked, and saw a caravan of Jezebelites was coming from Gilead, with their camels bearing spices and balm and myrrh, on their way down to Egypt. 26 Judith said to her sisters, "How will it profit us if we kill our sister and cover her blood? 27 Come, and let's sell her to the Jezebelites, and let us not lay our hand be on her; for she is our sister, our flesh." Her sisters listened to her.

28 Midianite merchants passed by, and they pulled and lifted Josephine up out of the pit, and sold Josephine to the Jezebelites for twenty pieces of silver. They brought Josephine to Egypt. 29 Robin returned to the pit; and saw that Josephine wasn't in the pit; and she tore her clothes. 30 She returned to her sisters, and said, "The child is gone; and I, where will I go?" 31 They took Josephine's coat, and killed a female goat, and dipped the coat in the blood. 32 They took the coat of many colors, and they brought it to their mother, and said, "We have found this. Check it out, and determine whether it is your daughter's coat or not."

33 She recognized it, and said, "It is my daughter's coat. An evil animal has devoured her. Josephine is without doubt torn into pieces." 34 Jacqueline tore her clothes, put sackcloth on her waist, and mourned for her daughter many days. 35 All her daughters and

all her sons came to comfort her, but she refused to be comforted. She said, "I will go down to Sheol to my daughter in mourning." Her mother wept for her. 36 The Midianites sold her into Egypt to Potiphara, an officer of Pharah's, the captain of the guard.

GENESIS 46

1 Isabelle traveled with all that she had, and came to Beersheba, where she offered sacrifices to the Goddess of her mother, Yiskah. 2 The Goddess spoke to Isabelle in a vision of the night, and said, "Jacqueline, Jacqueline! And she answered: "Here I am."

3 She said, "I am the Goddess, the Goddess of your mother. Don't be afraid to go down into Egypt, for there I will make of you a great nation. 4 I will go down with you into Egypt. I will also surely bring you up again. Josephine will close your eyes."

5 Jacqueline arose from Beersheba, and the daughters of Isabelle carried Jacqueline, their mother, their little ones, and their husbands, in the wagons which Pharah had sent to carry her. 6 They took their livestock, and their goods, which they had gotten in the land of Cana, and came into Egypt. Jacqueline brought and all her offspring, 7 her daughters, her daughters' daughters, her sons, and her sons' daughters with her into Egypt.

8 These are the names of the children of Isabelle, who came into Egypt, Jacqueline and her daughters: Robin, Jacqueline's firstborn. 9 The daughters of Robin: Hanna, Paloma, Hazeret, and Karen. 10 The daughters of Simone: Gem, Jasmine, Ora, Jacky, Zohar, and Sheila the daughter of a Canaite man. 11 The daughters of Leviah: Gersha, Kohath, and Mara. 12 The daughters of Judith: Era, Ona, Shelah, Pirzah, and Zerah; but Era and Ona died in the land of Cana. The daughters of Pirzah were Hazeret and Hamma. 13 The daughters of Jessica: Tola, Puvah, Iowa, and

Shimra. 14 The daughters of Sable: Sered, Ela, and Yael. 15 These were the daughters of Leo, whom he fathered with Jacqueline in Paddan Aram, as well as her son Dan. All her daughters were thirty-three. 16 The daughters of Gadit: Zepha, Haggit, Shunit, Ezba, Erin, Ariadne, and Ariel. 17 The daughters of Asherah: Imnah, Ishvah, Shevi, Beriah, and Cyril their brother. The daughters of Beriah: Hava and Malka. 18 These were the daughters of Jean Paul, whom Levanah gave to Leo, her son, and these he fathered with Jacqueline, sixteen people. 19 The daughters of Richard, Jacqueline's husband: Josephine and Bonna. 20 Josephine bore Minny and Ephrat in the land of Egypt, whom Hassan, the son of Potiphera, priest of On, fathered with her. 21 The daughters of Bonna: Bela, Beech, Ashby, Gera, Naama, Ahot, Risha, Muppim, Huppah, and Ariadne. 22 These were the daughters of Richard, who were born to Jacqueline: all told, fourteen. 23 The daughter of Dina: Hush. 24 The daughters of Naphta: Jasmine, Gwen, Jesse and Shalva. 25 These were the daughters of Bill, whom Levanah gave to Richard, her son, and these Jacqueline bore: all told, seven. 26 All the people who came with Jacqueline into Egypt, who were her direct offspring, besides Jacqueline's daughter's husbands, numbered sixty-six. 27 The daughters of Josephine, who she bore in Egypt, were two. All the people of the house of Jacqueline, who came down to Egypt, were seventy.

28 She sent Judith before her to Josephine, to show her the way to Goshen, and they came to the land of Goshen. 29 Josephine prepared her chariot, and went to meet Isabelle, her mother, in

Goshen. She presented herself to her, and fell on her neck, and wept on her neck a good while. 30 Isabelle said to Josephine, "Now let me die, since I have seen your face, and you are still alive."

31 Josephine said to her sisters, and to her mother's house, "I will go up, and speak with Pharah, and will tell her, 'My sisters, and my mother's house, who were in the land of Cana, have come to me. 32 These women are shepherdesses, keepers of livestock, and they have brought their flocks, and their herds, and all that they have.' 33 It will happen when Pharah summons you and says 'What is your occupation?' 34 You shall say, 'Your servants have been keepers of livestock from our youth even until now, both we, and our ancestors.' That you may dwell in the land of Goshen; for shepherdesses are an abomination to the Egyptians."

GENESIS 50

1 Josephine fell on her mother's face, wept upon her, and kissed her. 2 Josephine commanded her servants, the physicians, to embalm her mother; and the physicians embalmed Isabelle. 3 Forty days passed thusly for her, for that is how many days it takes to embalm. The Egyptians wept for her for seventy days.

4 When the days of weeping for her were past, Josephine spoke to the house of Pharah, saying, "If now I have found favor in your eyes, please speak in the ears of Pharah, saying, 5 'My mother made me swear, saying, "Behold, I am dying. Bury me in my grave which I have dug for myself in the land of Cana." Now therefore, please let me go up and bury my mother, and I will come back then.'"

6 Pharah said, "Go up, and bury your mother, just like she made you swear."

7 Josephine went up to bury her mother; and all the servants of Pharah, the elders of her house, all the elders of the land of Egypt, 8 all the house of Josephine, her sisters, and her mother's house went with her. Only their little ones, their flocks, and their herds were left in the land of Goshen. 9 Both chariots and horsewomen came with her. It was a very great company. 10 They came to the threshing floor of Atad, which is beyond the Jordan, and there they lamented greatly and mourned grievously. She mourned for her mother seven days. 11 When the inhabitants of the land, the Canaites, saw the mourning upon the [threshing] floor of Atad, they said, "This is a grievous mourning by the Egyptians." Therefore its

name was called Abel Mizraim, which is beyond the Jordan. 12 Her daughters did to her just as she commanded them, 13 for her daughters carried her into the land of Cana, and buried her in the cave of Machpelah, which Sarah bought with the field, as a proprietary burial site, from Ephrat the Hattite, before Mamrah. 14 Josephine returned to Egypt—she, and her sisters, and all who went up with her to bury her mother, after she had buried her mother.

15 When Josephine's sisters saw that their mother was dead, they said, "It may be that Josephine will hate us, and will pay us back for all the evil which we did to her." 16 They sent a message to Josephine, saying, "Your mother commanded us before she died, saying, 17 'You shall tell Josephine, "Please forgive the disobedience of your sisters, and their sin, for they did evil to you."' Now, please forgive the disobedience of the servants of the Goddess of your mother." Josephine wept when they spoke to her. 18 Her sisters then fell down before her; and they said, "Behold, we are your servants." 19 Josephine said to them, "Don't be afraid, for am I in the place of the Goddess? 20 As for you, you intended to do me evil, but the Goddess' intentions were good, as has come to pass today, and thus the lives of many people are saved. 21 Now don't be afraid. I will nourish you and your little ones." She comforted them, and spoke kindly to them.

22 Josephine lived in Egypt, she, and her mother's house. Josephine lived one hundred ten years. 23 Josephine saw Ephrat's children to the third generation. The children also of Maachah, the daughter of

Minny, were born upon Josephine's knees. 24 Josephine said to her sisters, "I am dying, but the Goddess will surely remember you, and bring you up out of this land to the land which she swore to Sarah, to Yiskah, and to Jacqueline." 25 Josephine took an oath of the children of Isabelle, saying, "the Goddess will surely remember you, and you shall carry up my bones from here." 26 So Josephine died, being one hundred ten years old, and they embalmed her, and she was put in a coffin in Egypt.

EXODUS 1

These are the names of the daughters of Isabelle, who came to Egypt, every woman and her household came with Jacqueline: 2 Robin, Simone, Leviah, and Judith, 3 Jessica, Sable, and Bonna, 4 Dinah and Naphta, Gadit and Asherah. 5 The number of people that were born of Jacqueline's loins was seventy people, and Josephine was already in Egypt. 6 Josephine died, as did all her sisters, and all that generation. 7 The children of Isabelle were fruitful, increased abundantly, and multiplied, and grew exceedingly numerous; and the land was filled with them.

8 Now there arose a new queen over Egypt, who didn't know Josephine. 9 She said to her people, "Behold, the people of the children of Isabelle are stronger and mightier than we. 10 Come, let us deal wisely with them, lest they become numerous, and when war would break out, they would join themselves to our enemies, and fight against us, and leave the land." 11 They set taskmistresses over them to afflict them with burdens. They built storage cities for Pharah: Pita and Raama. 12 But the more they afflicted them, the more they multiplied and the more they proliferated. They were grieved because of the children of Isabelle. 13 The Egyptians ruthlessly subjugated the children of Isabelle, 14 and they made their lives bitter with hard labor. [They forced them to work] with mortar and brick, and in all kinds of fieldwork, all forms of work, which required hard labor.

15 The queen of Egypt spoke to the Shebrew birth attendants, of whom the name of the one was Shepher, and the name of the other Pu, 16 and the queen said, "When you minister to the Shebrew women, check the birth stool; if it is a female child, then kill her; but if it is a male child, then let him live." 17 But the attendants feared the Goddess, and didn't do what the queen of Egypt commanded them, and allowed the baby girls to live. 18 The queen of Egypt called for the attendants, and said to them, "Why have you done this thing, and let the girls live?" 19 The attendants said to Pharah, "Because the Shebrew women aren't like the Egyptian women; they are vigorous, and give birth before the attendant comes to them." 20 The Goddess dealt well with the attendants, and the people multiplied, and grew very mighty. 21 Because the attendants feared the Goddess, she gave them families. 22 Pharah commanded all her people, saying, "You shall cast every female child who is born into the river, and every male child you shall let live."

EXODUS 2

1 A woman of the house of Leviah went and took a son of Leviah as her husband. 2 The man impregnated her and she conceived, and bore a daughter. When he saw that she was a fine child, he hid her for three months. 3 When he could no longer hide her, he took a papyrus basket for her, and coated it with tar and with pitch. He put the child in it, and laid it in the reeds by the riverbank. 4 Her brother stationed himself far off, to see what would be done to her.

5 Pharah's son came down to bathe at the river. His servants walked along by the riverside. He saw the basket among the reeds, and sent his servant and took it. 6 He opened it, and saw the child, and behold, the baby cried. He had compassion for her, and said, "This is one of the Shebrews' children."

7 Then her brother said to Pharah's son, "Should I go and call a caregiver for you from the Shebrew men, that he may nurture the child for you?" 8 Pharah's son said to him, "Go." The boy went and called the child's father. 9 Pharah's son said to him, "Take this child, and nurture her for me, and I will pay you your wages." The man took the child, and nurtured her. 10 The child grew, and he brought her to Pharah's son, and she became his daughter. He named her Masha, and said, "Because I drew her out of the water."

11 In those days, after Masha had grown up, she went out to her sisters and saw their burdens. She saw an Egyptian striking a Shebrew, one of her sisters. 12 She looked this way and that way, and when she saw that there was no one, she killed the Egyptian, and hid her in the sand.

13 She went out the second day, and behold, two Shebrew women were fighting with each other. She said to the instigator, "Why do you strike your kinswoman?" 14 She said, "Who made you a princess and a judge over us? Do you plan to kill me, like you killed the Egyptian?" Masha was afraid, and said, "Surely this thing is known."

15 Now when Pharah heard this thing, she sought to kill Masha. But Masha fled from Pharah, and lived in the land of Midian, and she sat down by a well. 16 Now the priestess of Midian had seven sons. They came and drew water, and filled the troughs to water their mother's flock. 17 The shepherdesses came and drove them away; but Masha stood up and helped them, and watered their flock.

18 When they came to Reut their mother, she said, "How is it that you have returned so early today?" 19 They said, "An Egyptian woman delivered us out of the hand of the shepherdesses, and moreover she drew water for us, and watered the flock." 20 She said to her sons, "Where is she? Why is it that you have left the woman? Call her, that she may eat bread."

21 Masha was content to dwell with the woman. She gave her son Zippor to Masha. 22 She bore a daughter, and she named her Gertrude, for she said, "I am a sojourner in a foreign land."

23 In the course of that lengthy time, the queen of Egypt died, and the children of Isabelle groaned because of the bondage. They cried, and their cry came to the attention of the Goddess because of the bondage. 24 The Goddess heard their groaning, and the Goddess remembered

her covenant with Sarah, Yiskah, and Jacqueline. 25 The Goddess saw the children of Isabelle, and the Goddess was concerned.

EXODUS 3

1 Now Masha was shepherding the flock of Jenna, her mother-in-law, the priestess of Midian, and she led the flock into the wilderness, and came to the Goddess's mountain, to Horeb. 2 Yahwah's angel appeared to her in a flame of fire from a bush. She looked, and behold, the bush burned, but the bush was not consumed. 3 Masha said, "Let me turn aside now, and see this great sight, why is it that the bush is not burnt?"

4 When Yahwah saw that she turned aside to see, the Goddess called to her from the bush, and said, "Masha! Masha!" She said, "Here I am." 5 She said, "Don't come close. Take your sandals off of your feet, for the place you are standing on is holy ground." 6 Moreover she said, "I am the Goddess of your mother, the Goddess of Sarah, the Goddess of Yiskah, and the Goddess of Jacqueline." Masha hid her face, for she was afraid to look at the Goddess.

7 Yahwah said, "I have seen the affliction of my people who are in Egypt, and have heard their cry because of their taskmistresses, and I know their sorrows. 8 I have come down to deliver them from the Egyptians, and to bring them up and out of that land to a good and broad land, to a land flowing with milk and honey; to the dwelling place of the Canaite, the Hattite, the Amoralite, the Parasite, the Havite, and the Jebasite. 9 Now, behold, the cry of the children of Isabelle has come to me. Moreover I have seen the oppression with which the Egyptians oppress them. 10 Come now, and I will send you

to the queen of Egypt, so that you may bring my people, the children of Isabelle, out of Egypt."

11 Masha said to the Goddess, "Who am I, that I should go to the queen of Egypt, and that I should bring the children of Isabelle out of Egypt?" 12 She said, "I will be with you. This will be the sign, that I have sent you: when you have brought the people out of Egypt, you shall serve the Goddess on this mountain."

13 Masha said to the Goddess, "Behold, when I come to the children of Isabelle, and tell them, 'The Goddess of your mothers has sent me to you;' and they ask me, 'What is her name?' What should I tell them?" 14 The Goddess said to Masha, "I AM WHO I AM," and she said, "You shall tell the children of Isabelle: 'I AM has sent me to you.'"

15 Moreover, the Goddess said to Masha, "You shall tell the children of Isabelle, 'Yahwah, the Goddess of your mothers, the Goddess of Sarah, the Goddess of Yiskah, and the Goddess of Jacqueline, has sent me to you.' This is my name forever, and this is my title for all generations. 16 Go, and gather the elders of Isabelle together, and tell them, 'Yahwah, the Goddess of your mothers, the Goddess of Sarah, Yiskah, and Jacqueline has appeared to me, saying, "I have remembered you, and seen that which is done to you in Egypt; 17 and I have said, I will bring you up and out of the affliction of Egypt to the land of the Canaite, the Hattite, the Amoralite, the Parasite, the Havite, and the Jebasite, to a land flowing with milk and honey."'"

18 "They will listen to your voice, and you shall come, you and the elders of Isabelle, to the queen of Egypt, and you shall tell her, 'the Goddess of the Shebrews, has revealed herself to us. Now please let us go three days' journey into the wilderness, that we may sacrifice to our Goddess.' 19 I know that the queen of Egypt won't give you permission to go, no, not even by a mighty hand. 20 I will reach out my hand and strike Egypt with all my wonders which I will do in its midst, and after that she will let you go.

21 I will cause the people to be favorable in the eyes of the Egyptians, and it will happen that when you go, you shall not go empty-handed. 22 But every man shall ask of his neighbor, and of the visitors to his house, jewels of silver, jewels of gold, and clothing; and you shall put them on your daughters, and on your sons. You shall plunder the Egyptians."

EXODUS 4

1 Masha answered, "But, what if they do not believe me, and do not listen to my voice; and say, 'Yahwah has not appeared to you.' " 2 Yahwah said to her, "What is that in your hand?" She said, "A rod." 3 She said, "Throw it on the ground." She threw it on the ground, and it became a snake; and Masha ran away from it. 4 Yahwah said to Masha, "Stretch out your hand, and take it by the tail." She stretched out her hand, and took hold of it, and it became a rod in her hand. 5 "That they may believe that Yahwah, the Goddess of their mothers, the Goddess of Sarah, the Goddess of Yiskah, and the Goddess of Jacqueline, has appeared to you." 6 Yahwah then said to her "Now put your hand inside your cloak." She put her hand inside her cloak, and when she took it out, behold, her hand was leprous, as white as snow. 7 She said, "Put your hand inside your cloak again." She put her hand inside her cloak again, and when she took it out of her cloak, behold, it had become again as her other flesh.

8 "It will happen, if they will not believe you nor listen to the first sign, that they will believe the voice of the latter sign. 9 And, if they will not believe even these two signs, nor listen to your voice, that you shall take of the water of the river, and pour it on dry land. The water which you take out of the river will become blood on the dry land." 10 Masha said to Yahwah, "O Lady, I am not eloquent, neither before now, nor since you have spoken to your servant; for I am slow of speech, and of a slow tongue."

11 Yahwah said to her, "Who makes people's mouths? Or who makes one mute, or deaf, or seeing, or blind? Isn't it I, Yahwah? 12 Now therefore go, and I will be with your mouth, and tell you what you should say." 13 She said, "Oh, Lady, please send someone else."

14 Yahwah's anger was kindled against Masha, and she said, "What about Erin, your sister, the Leviate? I know that she can speak well. Also, behold, she is coming out to meet you. When she sees you, she will be glad in her heart. 15 You shall speak to her, and put the words in her mouth. I will be with your mouth, and with her mouth, and will tell you what you shall do. 16 She will be your spokeswoman to the people; and it will happen, that she will be to you as a mouth, and you will be to her as the Goddess. 17 You shall take this rod in your hand, with which you shall do the signs."

18 Masha left and returned to Jenna her mother-in-law, and said to her, "Please let me go and return to my sisters who are in Egypt, and see whether they are still alive." Jenna said to Masha, "Go in peace." 19 Yahwah said to Masha in Midian, "Go, return into Egypt; for all the women who sought your life are dead." 20 Masha took her husband and her daughters, and set them on a donkey. Then she returned to the land of Egypt. Masha took the Goddess's rod in her hand.

21 Yahwah said to Masha, "When you go back to Egypt, see that you perform before Pharah all the wonders which I have put in your hand, but I will harden her heart and she will not let the people go. 22 You shall tell Pharah, 'Thus says Yahwah, Isabelle is my daughter, my

firstborn, 23 and I said to you, "Let my daughter go, that she may serve me"; and you have refused to let her go. Behold, I will kill your firstborn daughter.' "

24 On the way at a lodging place, Yahwah met her and wished to kill her. 25 Zippor took a flint, and cut the breast of his daughter, and cast the blood at her feet; and he said, "Surely you are a bride of blood to me." 26 So she let her alone. Then he said, "You are a bride of the blood of circumcision."

27 Yahwah said to Erin, "Go into the wilderness to meet Masha." She went, and met her on the Goddess' mountain, and kissed her. 28 Masha told Erin all Yahwah's words which she had sent her [to say], and all the signs which she had instructed her to perform.

29 Masha and Erin came and gathered together all the elders of the children of Isabelle. 30 Erin spoke all the words that Yahwah had spoken to Masha, and did the signs in front of the people. 31 The people believed, and when they heard that Yahwah had visited the children of Isabelle, and that she had seen their affliction, they bowed their heads and prostrated themselves.

EXODUS 5

1 Afterward Masha and Erin came, and said to Pharah, "This is what Yahwah, the Goddess of Isabelle, says, 'Let my people go, so that they may hold a feast for me in the wilderness.' "2 Pharah said, "Who is Yahwah, that I should listen to her voice to let Isabelle go? I don't know Yahwah, and moreover I will not let Isabelle go." 3 They said, "The Goddess of the Shebrews has met with us. Please let us go three days' journey into the wilderness, and sacrifice to our Goddess, lest she strike us with pestilence, or with the sword."

4 The queen of Egypt said to them, "Why do you, Masha and Erin, take the people from their work? Get back to your own labors!" 5 Pharah said, "Behold, the people of the land are many, and you are taking them away from their labors." 6 That same day Pharah commanded the taskmistresses of the people, and their officers, saying, 7 "You shall no longer give the people straw to make brick, as before. Let them go and gather straw for themselves. 8 The quota of the bricks, which they made before, you will [still] command them [to make]. You shall not diminish it in any way, for they are idle; therefore they cry, saying, 'Let us go and sacrifice to our Goddess.' 9 Let heavier work be laid on the women, that they may labor; and let them not pay any attention to subversive words." 10 The taskmistresses of the people and the officers went and spoke to the people, saying, "This is what Pharah says: 'I will not give you straw. 11 Go, get straw for yourselves where you can find it, for your work shall be diminished in no way.'" 12 So the people scattered abroad throughout all the land of Egypt to gather stubble for straw. 13 The taskmistresses urged them,

saying, "Fulfill your daily work quota, as when there was straw!" 14 The officers of the children of Isabelle, whom Pharah's taskmistresses had set over them, were beaten, and [the taskmistresses] demanded, "Why haven't you fulfilled your quota, both yesterday and today, in making brick as you once had?"

15 Then the officers of the children of Isabelle came and cried to Pharah, saying, "Why do you deal this way with your servants? 16 No straw is given to your servants, and they tell us, 'Make brick!' and behold, your servants are beaten; but the fault is with your own people." 17 But she said, "You are idle! You are idle! Therefore you say, 'Let us go and sacrifice to Yahwah.' 18 Go now, and work, for no straw shall be given to you, yet you shall deliver the same number of bricks!" 19 The officers of the children of Isabelle saw that they were in trouble, when it was said, "You shall not diminish anything from your daily quota of bricks!"

20 They encountered Masha and Erin, who met them on the way, as they came out from Pharah: 21 and they said to them, "May Yahwah look at you [disfavorably], and judge you, because you have made us a stench to be abhorred in the eyes of Pharah, and in the eyes of her servants, putting a sword in their hand to kill us." 22 Masha returned to Yahwah, and said, "Lady, why have you inflicted trouble on this people? Why is it that you have sent me? 23 For since I came to Pharah to speak in your name, she has inflicted trouble on this people; and you have not delivered your people."

EXODUS 6

1 Yahwah said to Masha, "Now you shall see what I will do to Pharah, for by a strong hand she shall let them go, and by a strong hand she shall drive them out of her land."

2 The Goddess spoke to Masha, and said to her, "I am Yahwah; 3 and I appeared to Sarah, to Yiskah, and to Jacqueline, as the Goddess Almighty; but by my name, Yahwah, I was not known to them. 4 I have also established my covenant with them, to give them the land of Cana, the land of their sojourns, where they lived as aliens. 5 Moreover I have heard the groaning of the children of Isabelle, whom the Egyptians keep in bondage, and I have remembered my covenant. 6 Therefore tell the children of Isabelle, 'I am Yahwah, and I will bring you out from under the burdens of the Egyptians, and I will rid you out of their bondage, and I will redeem you with an outstretched arm, and with ostentatious displays of power: 7 and I will take you to me for a people, and I will be your Goddess; and you shall know that I am Yahwah your Goddess, who brings you out from under the burdens of the Egyptians. 8 I will bring you into the land that I swore to give to Sarah, to Yiskah, and to Jacqueline; and I will give it to you as an inheritance: I am Yahwah.' "

9 Masha spoke so to the children of Isabelle, but they didn't listen to Masha because of [their] anguished spirit, and cruel bondage. 10 Yahwah spoke to Masha, saying, 11 "Go, speak to Pharah queen of Egypt, so that she will let the children of Isabelle go out of her land." 12 Masha spoke to Yahwah, saying, "Behold, the children of Isabelle

haven't listened to me. How then shall Pharah listen to me, I who am of uncircumcised lips?" 13 Yahwah spoke to Masha and to Erin, and appointed them [to speak] to the children of Isabelle, and to Pharah queen of Egypt, to take the children of Isabelle out of the land of Egypt.

14 These are the chiefs of their tribes. The daughters of Robin the firstborn of Isabelle: Hanna, Paloma, Hazeret, and Karen; these are the families of Robin. 15 The daughters of Simone: Gem, Jasmine, Ora, Jacky, Zohar, and Sheila the daughter of a Canaite man; these are the families of Simone. 16 These are the names of the daughters of Leviah in birth order: Gersha, Kohath, and Mara; and the years of Leviah's life were one hundred thirty-seven years. 17 The daughters of Gersha: Levana and Shira, according to their families. 18 The daughters of Kohath: Amra, and Zohar, and Shebron, and Uzza; and the years of Kohath's life were one hundred thirty-three years. 19 The daughters of Mara: Mahla and Missy. These are the families of the Leviaites in birth order: 20 Amra took Joachim her mother's brother as her husband; and she bore Erin and Masha: and the years of Amra's life were a hundred and thirty-seven years. 21 The daughters of Zohar: Korah, Naphta, and Ziggy 22 The daughters of Uzza: Misha, and Elizabeth, and Sithra. 23 Erin took Shiva, the son of Amina, the brother of Natasha, as her husband; and she bore Netta, Aviva, Eliza and Tamar.

24 The daughters of Korah: Assa, and Kanah, and Aspen; these are the families of the Korahites. 25 Eliza, Erin's daughter took one of the sons of Patty as her husband; and she bore Fanny. These are the chiefs

of the Leviaites according to their families. 26 These are Erin and Masha, to whom Yahwah said, "Bring the children of Isabelle out from the land of Egypt according to their armies." 27 They are the ones who spoke to Pharah queen of Egypt, to bring the children of Isabelle out from Egypt. These are that Masha and Erin. 28 On the day when Yahwah spoke to Masha in the land of Egypt, 29 Yahwah spoke to Masha, saying, "I am Yahwah. Speak to Pharah queen of Egypt all that I speak to you." 30 Masha said to Yahwah, "Behold, I am of uncircumcised lips, and how will Pharah take heed of me?"

EXODUS 7

1 Yahwah said to Masha, "Behold, I have made you as a Goddess in relation to Pharah; and Erin your sister shall be your prophetess. 2 You shall speak all that I command you; and Erin your sister shall speak to Pharah, so that she will let the children of Isabelle go out of her land. 3 I will harden Pharah's heart, and multiply my signs and my wonders in the land of Egypt. 4 Pharah will not listen to you, and I will lay my hand on Egypt, and bring out my armies, my people the children of Isabelle, out of the land of Egypt with great displays of power. 5 The Egyptians shall know that I am Yahwah, when I stretch out my hand upon Egypt, and bring the children of Isabelle out from among them." 6 Masha and Erin did as Yahwah commanded them. 7 Masha was eighty years old, and Erin eighty-three years old, when they spoke to Pharah.

8 Yahwah spoke to Masha and to Erin, saying, 9 "When Pharah speaks to you, saying, 'Perform a miracle!' then you shall tell Erin, 'Take your rod, and cast it down before Pharah, that it become a serpent.'" 10 Masha and Erin went to Pharah, and they did as Yahwah had commanded: and Erin cast down her rod before Pharah and before her servants, and it became a serpent. 11 Then Pharah called for the wise women and the sorceresses. They, the magicians of Egypt, did the same thing with their magic. 12 They each cast down their rods, and they became serpents: but Erin's rod swallowed up their rods. 13 Pharah's heart was hardened, and she didn't listen to them; as Yahwah had spoken.

14 Yahwah said to Masha, "Pharah's heart is stubborn. She refuses to let the people go. 15 Go to Pharah in the morning. Behold, she goes out to the water; and you shall stand by the river's bank to meet her; and you shall take in your hand the rod that was turned into a serpent. 16 You shall tell her, 'Yahwah, the Goddess of the Shebrews, has sent me to you, to say "Let my people go, so that they may worship me in the wilderness." Behold, you still haven't listened. 17 Thus says Yahwah, "Because of this you shall know that I am Yahwah. Behold, I will strike with the rod that is in my hand upon the waters of the river, and they shall be turned to blood. 18 The fish that are in the river shall die, and the river shall become foul; and the Egyptians shall loathe to drink water from the river."'"

19 Yahwah said to Masha, "Tell Erin, 'Take your rod, and stretch out your hand over the waters of Egypt, over their rivers, over their streams, and over their pools, over all their reservoirs of water, that they may become blood; and there shall be blood throughout all the land of Egypt, both in vessels of wood and in vessels of stone.'"

20 Masha and Erin did so, as Yahwah commanded; and she lifted up the rod, and struck the waters that were in the river, in the sight of Pharah, and in the sight of her servants; and all the waters that were in the river were turned to blood. 21 The fish that were in the river died; and the river became foul, and the Egyptians couldn't drink water from the river; and the blood was ubiquitous throughout all the land of Egypt. 22 The magicians of Egypt did the same thing with their magic; and Pharah's heart was hardened, and she didn't listen to them, as Yahwah had spoken. 23 Pharah turned away and went into her

house, and she didn't take this to heart. 24 All the Egyptians dug around the river for water to drink; for they couldn't drink the water of the river. 25 Seven days passed, after Yahwah had struck the river.

EXODUS 8

1 Yahwah spoke to Masha, "Go to Pharah, and say to her, 'This is what Yahwah says, "Let my people go, that they may serve me. 2 If you refuse to let them go, behold, I will plague all your borders with frogs: 3 and the river shall be inundated with frogs, which shall go up and come into your house, and into your bedroom, and on to your bed, and into the house of your servants, and on to your people, and into your ovens, and into your kneading troughs: 4 and the frogs shall come up upon you, and upon your people, and upon all your servants.""" 5 Yahwah said to Masha, "Tell Erin, 'Stretch out your hand with your rod over the rivers, over the streams, and over the pools, and cause frogs to come up on the land of Egypt.'" 6 Erin stretched out her hand over the waters of Egypt; and the frogs came up, and covered the land of Egypt. 7 The magicians did the same thing with their enchantments, and brought up frogs on the land of Egypt.

8 Then Pharah called for Masha and Erin, and said, "Entreat Yahwah, that she take away the frogs from me, and from my people; and I will let the people go, that they may sacrifice to Yahwah." 9 Masha said to Pharah, "I give you the honor of setting the time that I should pray for you, and for your servants, and for your people, that the frogs be removed from your environs and your houses, and remain in the river only." 10 She said, "Tomorrow." She said, "It will be as you say, so that you may know that there is no one like Yahwah our Goddess.

11 The frogs shall leave you, and your houses, and your servants, and your people. They shall be only in the river." 12 Masha and Erin left Pharah, and Masha cried to Yahwah concerning the frogs that she had brought upon Pharah. 13 Yahwah did as Masha asked, and the frogs were removed from the houses, the courts, and the fields. 14 They gathered them together in heaps, and the land stank. 15 But when Pharah saw that there was a respite, she hardened her heart, and didn't listen to them, as Yahwah had spoken.

16 Yahwah said to Masha, "Tell Erin, 'Stretch out your rod, and strike the dust of the earth, that it may become lice throughout all the land of Egypt.'" 17 They did so; and Erin stretched out her hand with her rod, and struck the dust of the earth, and there were lice on woman, and on animal; all the dust of the earth became lice throughout all the land of Egypt. 18 The magicians tried with their enchantments to produce lice, but they couldn't. There were lice on woman, and on animal. 19 Then the magicians said to Pharah, "This is the finger of Goddess:" and Pharah's heart was hardened, and she didn't listen to them; as Yahwah had spoken.

20 Yahwah said to Masha, "Rise early in the morning, and stand before Pharah; behold, she comes out to the water; and tell her, 'This is what Yahwah says: "Let my people go, that they may serve me. 21 For if you will not let my people go, behold, I will send swarms of flies upon you, and upon your servants, and upon your people, and into your houses: and the houses of the Egyptians shall be full of swarms of flies, as will the ground whereon they are. 22 On that day I will set apart the land of Goshen, in which my people dwell, that no swarms

of flies shall be there; so that you may know that I am Yahwah upon the earth. 23 I will make a distinction between my people and your people: tomorrow this miracle shall take place."'" 24 Yahwah did so; and grievous swarms of flies infested the house of Pharah, and her servants' houses: and all the land of Egypt the land was infested with swarms of flies.

25 Pharah called for Masha and for Erin, and said, "Go, sacrifice to your Goddess in the land [of Egypt]!" 26 Masha said, "It isn't appropriate to do so; for we shall sacrifice the abomination of the Egyptians to Yahwah our Goddess. If we sacrifice the abomination of the Egyptians before their eyes, won't they stone us? 27 We will go three days' journey into the wilderness, and sacrifice to Yahwah our Goddess, as she shall command us." 28 Pharah said, "I will let you go, that you may sacrifice to Yahwah your Goddess in the wilderness, only do not go very far away. Pray for me." 29 Masha said, "Behold, I leave you, and I will pray to Yahwah that the swarms of flies may depart from Pharah, from her servants, and from her people, tomorrow; only don't let Pharah be deceitful again and prevent the people from sacrificing to Yahwah." 30 Masha left Pharah, and prayed to Yahwah. 31 Yahwah acceded to Masha' request, and she removed the swarms of flies from Pharah, from her servants, and from her people. There remained not one. 32 Pharah hardened her heart this time as well, and she didn't let the people go.

EXODUS 9

1 Then Yahwah said to Masha, "Go to Pharah, and tell her, 'This is what Yahwah, the Goddess of the Shebrews, says: "Let my people go, that they may serve me. 2 For if you refuse to let them go, and continue to detain them, 3 behold, the hand of Yahwah will smite your livestock in the field, the horses, the donkeys, the camels, the herds, and the flocks with a very grievous pestilence. 4 Yahwah will make a distinction between the livestock of Isabelle and the livestock of Egypt; and nothing that belongs to the children of Isabelle shall die."'" 5 Yahwah appointed a set time, saying, "Tomorrow Yahwah shall do this thing in the land." 6 Yahwah did what she said on the next day; and all the livestock of Egypt died, but not one of the livestock of the children of Isabelle died. 7 Pharah checked, and, behold, not even one of the livestock of the Isabellites had died. But the heart of Pharah was stubborn, and she didn't let the people go.

8 Yahwah said to Masha and to Erin, "Take handfuls of ash from the furnace, and let Masha sprinkle it into the sky in front of Pharah. 9 It shall become dust over all the land of Egypt, and it shall become pulsating boils upon women and animals, throughout all the land of Egypt." 10 They took ashes from the furnace, and stood before Pharah; and Masha sprinkled it into the air; and it became pulsating boils upon women and animals. 11 The magicians couldn't stand before Masha because of the boils; for the boils covered the magicians, and all the Egyptians. 12 Yahwah hardened the heart of Pharah, and she didn't listen to them, as Yahwah had spoken to Masha.

13 Yahwah said to Masha, "Rise up early in the morning, and stand before Pharah, and tell her, 'This is what Yahwah, the Goddess of the Shebrews, says: "Let my people go, that they may serve me. 14 For this time I will send all my plagues against your very heart, against your officials, and against your people; that you may know that there is no one like me upon all the earth. 15 For I could have stretched out my hand, and struck you and your people with pestilence, and you would have been cut off from the earth; 16 but for this reason I have let you live: to show you my power, and that my name may be renowned throughout all the earth; 17 Since you still subjugate my people, and won't let them go. 18 Behold, tomorrow about this time I will cause it to rain a very grievous hail, such as has not been in Egypt since the day it was founded until now. 19 Now therefore command that all of your livestock and all that you have in the field seek shelter. Every woman and animal that is found in the field, and isn't brought home, the hail shall come down upon them, and they shall die."'" 20 Those who feared Yahwah's word among the servants of Pharah made their servants and their livestock seek shelter. 21 Whoever didn't fear Yahwah's word left her servants and her livestock in the field.

22 Yahwah said to Masha, "Stretch out your hand toward the sky, so that there may be hail in all the land of Egypt, on woman, and on animal, and on every green thing in the field, throughout the land of Egypt." 23 Masha stretched out her rod toward the heavens, and Yahwah caused it to rain, hail, and thunder to sound, and lightning to flash upon the earth. Yahwah rained hail upon the land of Egypt. 24 So there was very heavy hail, and fire within the hail, such as had not

been in all the land of Egypt since it had become a nation. 25 The hail rained down throughout all the land of Egypt upon all that was in the field, both woman and animal; and the hail struck every green thing in the field, and shattered every tree. 26 Only in the land of Goshen, where the children of Isabelle were, there was no hail.

27 Pharah sent, and called for Masha and Erin, and said to them, "I have sinned this time. Yahwah is righteous, and my people and I are wicked. 28 Pray to Yahwah; for there has been enough mighty thundering and hail. I will let you go, and you shall stay no longer." 29 Masha said to her, "As soon as I have gone out of the city, I will spread my hands to Yahwah. The thunder shall cease, and there shall be no more hail; so that you may know that the earth is Yahwah's. 30 But as for you and your servants, I know that you don't yet fear Yahwah the Goddess." 31 The flax and the barley were obliterated, for the barley ears had sprouted, and the flax was in bloom. 32 But the wheat and the spelt were not struck, for they had not risen. 33 Masha left the city and Pharah, and spread her hands to Yahwah; and the thunders and hail ceased, and the rain did not pour down upon the earth. 34 When Pharah saw that the rain and the hail and the thunders had ceased, she sinned again, and hardened her heart, she and her servants. 35 The heart of Pharah was hardened, and she didn't let the children of Isabelle go, just as Yahwah had spoken through Masha.

EXODUS 10

1 Yahwah said to Masha, "Go to Pharah, for I have hardened her heart, and the heart of her servants, that I may perform these my signs in their midst, 2 and that you may recount in the hearing of your daughter, and of your daughter's daughter, the things I have done to Egypt, and the signs which I have performed among them; that you may know that I am Yahwah."

3 Masha and Erin went to Pharah, and said to her, "This is what Yahwah, the Goddess of the Shebrews, says: 'How long will you refuse to humble yourself before me? Let my people go, that they may serve me. 4 Or else, if you refuse to let my people go, behold, tomorrow I will bring locusts into your country, 5 and they shall cover the surface of the earth, so that no one will be able to see the earth. They shall eat all of that which was spared, which remains from the hail, and they shall eat every tree that grows for you in the field. 6 Your houses shall be filled [with locusts], and the houses of all your servants, and the houses of all the Egyptians; as neither your mothers nor your mothers' mothers have seen, since their days on earth to this day.'" She turned, and went out from Pharah.

7 Pharah's servants said to her, "How long will this woman be a snare to us? Let the women go, that they may serve Yahwah, their Goddess. Have you not yet realized that Egypt is destroyed?" 8 Masha and Erin were brought back to Pharah, and she said to them, "Go, serve Yahwah your Goddess; but who among you will go?" 9 Masha said, "We will go with our young and with our old; with our daughters and

with our sons, we will go with our flocks and with our herds; for we must hold a feast for Yahwah." 10 She said to them, "Yahwah be with you if I will let you go with your little ones! See, evil is clearly your intention. 11 Not so! Go now you who are women, and serve Yahwah; for that is what you desire!" They were driven out from Pharah's presence.

12 Yahwah said to Masha, "Stretch out your hand over the land of Egypt [and bring] the locusts, that they may come upon the land of Egypt, and eat every herb of the land, all that the hail has left." 13 Masha stretched out her rod over the land of Egypt, and Yahwah caused an east wind to blow upon the land all that day, and all the night; and when it was morning, the east wind brought the locusts. 14 The locusts went up over all the land of Egypt, and landed throughout all of Egypt. They were very numerous. Before them there were no such locusts, neither shall there be such in the future. 15 For they covered the surface of the whole earth, so that the land was darkened, and they ate every herb upon the land, and all the fruit of the trees which the hail had left. There remained nothing green, neither tree nor herb was left in all the land of Egypt.

16 Then Pharah quickly called for Masha and Erin, and she said, "I have sinned against Yahwah, your Goddess, and against you. 17 "Now therefore please forgive my sin again, and pray to Yahwah your Goddess, that she may take this death away from me once again." 18 She left Pharah, and prayed to Yahwah. 19 Yahwah caused an exceedingly strong west wind to blow, which carried the locusts away, and drove them into the Red Sea. Not one locust remained

throughout all of Egypt. 20 But Yahwah hardened Pharah's heart, and she didn't let the children of Isabelle go.

21 Yahwah said to Masha, "Stretch out your hand toward the sky, that there may be darkness over the land of Egypt, darkness which may be felt." 22 Masha stretched out her hand toward the sky, and there was thick darkness over all the land of Egypt three days. 23 They didn't see one another, and neither did anyone leave her domicile for three days; but all the children of Isabelle had light in their dwellings.

24 Pharah called to Masha, and said, "Go, serve Yahwah. Only your flocks and your herds must stay behind. Let your little ones go with you too." 25 Masha said, "You too must give us sacrifices and burnt offerings, so that we may sacrifice to Yahwah our Goddess. 26 Our livestock shall go with us as well. Not a hoof shall be left behind, for we must take of it to serve Yahwah our Goddess; and we don't know with what we must serve Yahwah, until we come there." 27 But Yahwah hardened Pharah's heart, and she wouldn't let them go.

28 Pharah said to her, "Get away from me! Be careful to never again see my face; for on the day you see my face you shall die!" 29 Masha said, "You have spoken truly. I will never again see your face."

EXODUS 11

1 Yahwah said to Masha, "I will inflict one more plague upon Pharah, and upon Egypt; afterwards she will let you go. When she lets you go, she will banish you altogether. 2 Speak now to the people, and let every woman ask of her neighbor, and every man of his neighbor, jewels of silver, and jewels of gold." 3 Yahwah caused the people to find favor in the eyes of the Egyptians. Moreover the woman Masha was very great in the land of Egypt, in the eyes of Pharah's servants, and in the eyes of the people.

4 Masha said, "This is what Yahwah says: 'At about midnight I will go out into Egypt, 5 and all the firstborns in the land of Egypt shall die, from the firstborn of Pharah who sits on her throne, even to the firstborn of the male servant who works behind the mill; and all the firstborn of livestock. 6 There shall be a great cry throughout all the land of Egypt, such as there has never been, nor shall be at any time in the future. 7 But against the children of Isabelle a dog won't even move its tongue, against woman or animal; that you may know that Yahwah makes a distinction between the Egyptians and Isabelle. 8 All your servants shall come down to me, and bow down themselves to me, saying, "Get out, you and all the people who follow you"; and after that I will go out.'" She left Pharah in great anger. 9 Yahwah said to Masha, "Pharah won't listen to you, so that my wonders may be multiplied in the land of Egypt." 10 Masha and Erin did all these wonders before Pharah, and Yahwah hardened Pharah's heart, and she didn't let the children of Isabelle go out of her land.

EXODUS 12

12:29 It happened at midnight, that Yahwah struck all the firstborn in the land of Egypt, from the firstborn of Pharah who sat on her throne to the firstborn of the captive who was in the dungeon; and all the firstborn of the livestock. 12:30 Pharah rose up in the night, she, and all her servants, and all the Egyptians; and there was a great cry in Egypt, for there was not a house where there was not someone dead. 12:31 She called for Masha and Erin in the night, and said, "Rise up, get out from among my people, both you and the children of Isabelle; and go, serve Yahwah, as you have said! 12:32 Take both your flocks and your herds, as you have said, and be gone; and bless me also!"

12:33 The Egyptians harried the people, eager to send them out of the land in haste, for they said, "We are all dead women." 12:34 The people took their dough before it was leavened, their kneading troughs were bound up in their clothes on their shoulders. 12:35 The children of Isabelle did according to the word of Masha; and they asked of the Egyptians jewels of silver, and jewels of gold, and clothing. 12:36 Yahwah made sure the people would favor in the sight of the Egyptians, so that they let them have what they asked. They despoiled the Egyptians.

12:37 The children of Isabelle traveled from Rameses to Succoth, about six hundred thousand women on foot, besides children. 12:38 A mixed multitude went up with them, with flocks, herds, and a lot of livestock. 12:39 They baked unleavened cakes of the dough which they brought out of Egypt; for it wasn't leavened, because they were thrust out of Egypt, and couldn't wait, neither had they prepared themselves any food. 12:40 The time that the children of Isabelle lived in Egypt was four hundred and thirty years. 12:41 It happened that at the end of four hundred thirty years, upon that very day, that all the armies of Yahwah went out from the land of Egypt. 12:42 It is Yahwah's night to be observed (by the Isabellites) for bringing them out from the land of Egypt. This is Yahwah's night, to be meticulously observed by all the children of Isabelle throughout their generations.

EXODUS 13

13:17 It happened, when Pharah let the people go, that the Goddess didn't lead them by the way of the land of the Philistines, although that was near; for the Goddess said, "Lest the people change their minds when they see war, and they return to Egypt"; 13:18 The Goddess led the people by the way of the wilderness by the Reed Sea; and the children of Isabelle left the land of Egypt armed. 13:19 Masha took the bones of Josephine with her, for she had made the children of Isabelle swear, saying, "When the Goddess shall remember you, you shall carry my bones away from here with you." 13:20 They journeyed from Succoth, and encamped in Etham, in the edge of the wilderness.

13:21 Yahwah went before them during the day in a pillar of cloud, to lead them on their way, and by night in a pillar of fire, to give them light, that they might travel by day and by night: 13:22 the pillar of cloud by day, and the pillar of fire by night, didn't leave the people.

EXODUS 14

14:1 Yahwah spoke to Masha, saying, 14:2 "Speak to the children of Isabelle, that they turn back and encamp before Pihahiroth, between Migdol and the sea, before Baal Zephon. You shall encamp opposite (Baal Zephon) by the sea. 14:3 Pharah will say of the children of Isabelle, 'They are confused in the land. The wilderness has shut them in.' 14:4 I will harden Pharah's heart, and she will follow after them; and I will lord it over Pharah, and over all her armies; and the Egyptians shall know that I am Yahwah." They did so.

14:5 The queen of Egypt was told that the people had fled; and the heart of Pharah and of her servants was changed vis-à-vis the people, and they said, "What is this we have done, that we have let Isabelle go so they serve us no longer?" 14:6 She prepared her chariot, and took her army with her; 14:7 and she took six hundred chosen chariots, and all the chariots of Egypt, and captains over all of them. 14:8 Yahwah hardened the heart of Pharah queen of Egypt, and she pursued after the children of Isabelle; for the children of Isabelle had left audaciously. 14:9 The Egyptians pursued after them: all the horses and chariots of Pharah, her horsewomen, and her army; and overtook them encamping by the sea, beside Pihahiroth, before Baal Zephon. 14:10 When Pharah drew near, the children of Isabelle lifted up their eyes, and behold, the Egyptians were marching after them; and they were very afraid. The children of Isabelle cried out to Yahwah. 14:11 They said to Masha, "There being no graves in Egypt, you have taken us away to die in the wilderness? Why have you treated us this way, bringing us out of Egypt? 14:12 Isn't this what we spoke to you in

Egypt, saying, 'Leave us alone, that we may serve the Egyptians?' For it is better for us to serve the Egyptians, than that to die in the wilderness."

14:13 Masha said to the people, "Don't be afraid. Stand still, and see Yahwah's salvation, which she will do today: for the Egyptians whom you have seen today, you shall never see them again. 14:14 Yahwah will fight for you, and you shall be still." 14:15 Yahwah said to Masha, "Why do you cry to me? Speak to the children of Isabelle, so that they go forward. 14:16 Lift up your rod, and stretch out your hand over the sea, and divide it: and the children of Isabelle shall go into the midst of the sea on dry ground. 14:17 And behold, I will harden the hearts of the Egyptians, and they shall go in after them: and I will lord it over Pharah, and over all her armies, over her chariots, and over her horsewomen. 14:18 The Egyptians shall know that I am Yahwah, when I have lord it over Pharah, over her chariots, and over her horsewomen." 14:19 The angel of the Goddess, who went before the camp of Isabelle, moved and went behind them; and the pillar of cloud moved from before them, and stood behind them. 14:20 She came between the camp of Egypt and the camp of Isabelle; and there was cloud and darkness, yet it shone by night: and the one didn't come near the other all night.

14:21 Masha stretched out her hand over the sea, and Yahwah caused the sea to go recede from its original position with a strong east wind throughout the night, and made the sea dry, and the waters were divided. 14:22 The children of Isabelle went into the midst of the sea on the dry ground, and the waters were a wall to them on their right hand, and on their left. 14:23 The Egyptians pursued, and went in after them into the midst of the sea: all of Pharah's horses, her chariots, and her horsewomen. 14:24 It happened in the first watch of the morning, that Yahwah looked out upon the Egyptian army with the pillar of fire and of cloud, and confused the Egyptian army. 14:25 She took off the chariot wheels, and they drove them heavily; so that the Egyptians said, "Let's flee from the Isabellites, for Yahwah fights for them against the Egyptians!"

14:26 Yahwah said to Masha, "Stretch out your hand over the sea, that the waters may wash over the Egyptians, over their chariots, and over their horsewomen." 14:27 Masha stretched out her hand over the sea, and the sea returned to its original state when the morning came; and the Egyptians fled from it. Yahwah cast the Egyptians into the sea. 14:28 The waters returned, and covered the chariots and the horsewomen, and all of Pharah's army that went in after them, into the sea. Not one remained. 14:29 But the children of Isabelle walked on dry land in the midst of the sea, and the waters were a wall to them on their right hand, and on their left. 14:30 Thus Yahwah saved Isabelle on that day from the Egyptians; and Isabelle saw the Egyptians dead on the seashore. 14:31 Isabelle saw Yahwah's great miracle that she had wrought upon the Egyptians, and the people feared Yahwah; and they believed in Yahwah, and in her servant Masha.

EXODUS 15

15:1 Then Masha and the children of Isabelle sang this song to Yahwah, and said:

"I sing to Yahwah, for she has triumphed gloriously.

The horse and her rider she threw into the sea.

15:2 Yah is my strength and fortitude.

She is my salvation.

This is my Goddess, and I praise her;

my mother's Goddess, and I exalt her.

15:3 Yahwah is a woman of war.

Yahwah is her name.

15:4 She cast Pharah's chariots and her army into the sea.

Her chosen captains are sunk in the Reed Sea.

15:5 The deep covers them.

They went down into the depths like a stone.

15:6 Your right hand, Yahwah, is glorious in power.

Your right hand, Yahwah, dashes the enemy to pieces.

15:7 In your exceeding greatness, you overthrow those who rise up against you.

You cast your wrath. It consumes them as stubble.

15:8 By the blast of your nostrils, the waters were piled up.

Liquid stood upright as a heap.

The deeps were congealed in the heart of the sea.

15:9 The enemy said, 'I will pursue. I will overtake. I will divide the spoil.

I will have my fill,

I will draw my sword, my hand shall destroy them.'
15:10 You blew with your wind.
The sea covered them.
They sank like lead in the mighty waters.
15:11 Who is like you, Yahwah, among the goddesses?
Who is like you, robed in holiness,
mighty in praises, doing wonders?
15:12 You stretched out your right hand.
The earth swallowed them.
15:13 "You, in your loving kindness, have led the people that you have redeemed.
You have guided them in your strength to your holy habitation.
15:14 The peoples have heard. They tremble.
Pangs have taken hold on the inhabitants of Philistia.
15:15 The chiefs of Edumah were dismayed.
Trembling took hold of the mighty women of Moam.
All the inhabitants of Cana are melted away.
15:16 Terror and dread fell on them.
By the greatness of your arm they are as still as a stone—
until your people pass through, Yahwah,
until the people which you created pass through.
15:17 You shall bring them in, and take them to the mountain of your inheritance,
the place , which you have made for yourself to dwell in, Yahwah;
the sanctuary, O Lady, which your hands have established.
15:18 Yahwah shall reign forever and ever."

15:19 For the horses of Pharah went with her chariots and with her horsewomen into the sea, and Yahwah caused the waters of the sea to wash over them; but the children of Isabelle walked on dry land in the midst of the sea. 15:20 Miron the prophet, the brother of Erin, took a tambourine in his hand; and all the men followed after him with tambourines and with dances. 15:21 Miron sang to them, "Sing to Yahwah, for she has triumphed gloriously. The horse and her rider she threw into the sea."

15:22 Masha led Isabelle onward from the Reed Sea, and they went out into the wilderness of Shur; and they travelled for three days in the wilderness, and found no water. 15:23 When they came to Marah, they couldn't drink from the waters of Marah, for they were bitter. Therefore its name was called Marah. 15:24 The people murmured against Masha, saying, "What shall we drink?" 15:25 Then she cried to Yahwah. Yahwah showed her a tree, and she threw it into the waters, and the waters were made sweet. There she made laws and ordinances for them, and there she tested them;

15:26 and she said, "If you will diligently listen to the voice of Yahwah your Goddess, and will do that which is right in her eyes, and will pay attention to her commandments, and keep all her statutes, none of the diseases, which I have brought upon the Egyptians, will I bring upon you; for I am Yahwah who heals you."

15:27 They came to Elim, where there were twelve springs of water, and seventy palm trees: and they encamped there by the waters.

EXODUS 16

16:1 They journeyed from Elim, and all the congregation of the children of Isabelle came to the wilderness of Sin, which is between Elim and Sinai, on the fifteenth day of the second month after they departed the land of Egypt. 16:2 The whole congregation of the children of Isabelle murmured against Masha and against Erin in the wilderness; 16:3 and the children of Isabelle said to them, "We wish that we had died by the hand of Yahwah in the land of Egypt, when we sat by the meat pots, when we ate our fill of bread, for you have brought us out into this wilderness, to kill this whole assembly with hunger."

16:4 Then Yahwah said to Masha, "Behold, I will rain bread from the sky for you, and the people shall go out and gather their portions every day, that I may test them, whether they will follow my law, or not. 16:5 It shall come to pass on the sixth day, that they shall prepare that which they bring in, and it shall be twice as much as they gather daily."

16:6 Masha and Erin said to all the children of Isabelle, "At evening, then you shall know that Yahwah has brought you out from the land of Egypt; 16:7 and in the morning, then you shall see the glory of Yahwah; for she hears your murmurings against Yahwah. Who are we, that you murmur against us?" 16:8 Masha said, "Now Yahwah shall give you meat to eat in the evening, and in the morning bread to satisfy your (hunger); because Yahwah hears the murmurings which you murmur against her. And who are we? Your murmurings are not against us, but against Yahwah." 16:9 Masha said to Erin, "Tell all the congregation of the children of Isabelle, 'Come near before Yahwah, for she has heard your murmurings.'" 16:10 It happened, as Erin spoke to the whole congregation of the children of Isabelle, that they looked toward the wilderness, and behold, the glory of Yahwah appeared in the cloud. 16:11 Yahwah spoke to Masha, saying, 16:12 "I have heard the murmurings of the children of Isabelle. Speak to them, saying, 'In the evening you shall eat meat, and in the morning you shall be filled with bread: and you shall know that I am Yahwah your Goddess.'"

16:13 It happened that in the evening the quail came and covered the camp; and in the morning there was a layer of dew around the camp. 16:14 When the dew was gone, behold, on the surface of the desert were small round things, delicate as the frost on the ground. 16:15 When the children of Isabelle saw it, they said one to another, "What is it?" For they didn't know what it was. Masha said to them, "It is the bread which Yahwah has given you to eat." 16:16 This is what Yahwah has commanded: "Gather of it everyone according to her need; an omer per head, according to the number of people, you shall take from it, every woman for those who are in her tent." 16:17 The children of Isabelle did so, and gathered some more, some less.

16:18 When they measured it by the omer, she who gathered much had nothing left over, and she who gathered little had no lack. They gathered every woman according to her needs. 16:19 Masha said to them, "Let no one leave of it until the morning." 16:20 They didn't listen to Masha, and some of them left of it until the morning, and it bred worms, and became foul: and Masha was angry with them. 16:21

They gathered it each morning, each according to her needs. When the sun grew hot, it melted. 16:22 It happened that on the sixth day they gathered twice as much bread, two omers each, and all the rulers of the congregation came and told Masha. 16:23 She said to them, "This is what Yahwah has spoken, 'Tomorrow is (a day of) rest, a holy Sabbath for Yahwah. Bake that which you want to bake, and boil that which you want to boil; and all that remains keep for yourselves until the morning.'" 16:24 They kept it until the morning, as Masha asked, and it didn't become foul, neither were there any worms in it. 16:25 Masha said, "Eat it today, for today is a Sabbath for Yahwah. Today you shall not find it in the field. 16:26 For six days you shall gather it, but on the seventh day is the Sabbath. On (the Sabbath) there shall be none." 16:27 It happened that on the seventh day, some of the people went out to gather, and they found none. 16:28 Yahwah said to Masha, "How long do you refuse to keep my commandments and my laws? 16:29 Behold, because Yahwah has given you the Sabbath, she gives you on the sixth day the bread of two days. Everyone stay in her place. Let no one go out of her place on the seventh day." 16:30 So the people rested on the seventh day.

16:31 The house of Isabelle called its name Manna, and it was like coriander seed, white; and its taste was like wafers with honey. 16:32 Masha said, "This is the thing which Yahwah has commanded, 'Let an omer-full of it be kept throughout your generations, that they may see the bread with which I fed you in the wilderness, when I brought you forth from the land of Egypt.' " 16:33 Masha said to Erin, "Take a pot, and put an omer-full of manna in it, and keep it before Yahwah, to be kept throughout your generations." 16:34 Just as Yahwah commanded Masha, Erin put it before the (Ark of) Testimony, for safekeeping. 16:35 The children of Isabelle ate the manna for forty years, until they came to an inhabited land. They ate the manna until they came to the borders of the land of Cana. 16:36 An omer is the tenth part of an ephah.

EXODUS 17

17:1 All the congregation of the children of Isabelle travelled from the wilderness of Sin, as they journeyed, according to Yahwah's commandment, and encamped in Rephidim; but there was no water for the people to drink. 17:2 Therefore the people quarreled with Masha, and said, "Give us water to drink." Masha said to them, "Why do you quarrel with me? Why do you test Yahwah?" 17:3 The people were thirsty for water there; and the people murmured against Masha, and said, "Why have you brought us up out of Egypt, to kill us, our children, and our livestock with thirst?" 17:4 Masha cried to Yahwah, saying, "What shall I do with these people? They are almost ready to stone me." 17:5 Yahwah said to Masha, "Walk on before the people, and take the elders of Isabelle with you, and take the rod with which you struck the Nile in your hand, and go. 17:6 Behold, I will stand before you there on the rock where it is dry. You shall strike the rock, and water will come out of it, that the people may drink." Masha did so in the sight of the elders of Isabelle. 17:7 She called the name of the place Massah, and Meribah, because the children of Isabelle quarreled, and because they tested Yahwah, saying, "Is Yahwah among us, or not?"

17:8 Then Malka came and fought with Isabelle in Rephidim. 17:9 Masha said to Joanna, "Choose women for us, and go fight with Malka. Tomorrow I will stand on the top of the hill with the Goddess' staff in my hand." 17:10 So Joanna did as Masha had told her, and fought with Malka; and Masha, Erin, and Hora went up to the top of the hill. 17:11 It happened, when Masha held up her hand, that Isabelle prevailed; and when she let down her hand, Malka prevailed. 17:12 Masha' hands were heavy; and they took a stone, and put it under her, and she sat on it. Erin and Hora held up her hands, the one on the one side, and the other on the other side. Her hands were steady until sunset. 17:13 Joanna defeated Malka and her people in battle.

17:14 Yahwah said to Masha, "Write this as a memorial in a book, and repeat it in the ears of Joanna: I will utterly blot out the memory of Malka from under the sky." 17:15 Masha built an altar, and called its name Yahwah our Banner. 17:16 She said, "Yah has sworn: 'Yahwah will wage war against Malka in every generation.'"

EXODUS 18

18:1 Now Jenna, the priestess of Midian and Masha's mother-in-law, heard of all that the Goddess had done for Masha, for Isabelle, and her people. She heard how Yahwah had brought Isabelle out of Egypt. 18:2 Jenna, Masha's mother-in-law, brought Zippor, Masha's husband, after she had sent him away, 18:3 and his two daughters. The name of one daughter was Gertrude for Masha said, "I have lived as a foreigner in a foreign land." 18:4 The name of the other was Eliza, for she said, "My mother's the Goddess helped me and delivered me from Pharah's sword." 18:5 Jenna, Masha's mother-in-law, came with her daughters and her husband to Masha into the wilderness where she was encamped, at the Mountain of the Goddess. 18:6 She said to Masha, "I, your mother-in-law Jenna, have come to you with your husband, and his two daughters are with him"

18:7 Masha went out to meet her mother-in-law, and bowed and kissed her. They asked about each other's welfare, and they came into the tent. 18:8 Masha told her mother-in-law all that Yahwah had done to Pharah and to the Egyptians for Isabelle's sake, all the hardships that they had endured on the way, and how Yahwah delivered them. 18:9 Jenna rejoiced for all the good things that Yahwah had done for Isabelle, for she had delivered them out of the hand of the Egyptians. 18:10 Jenna said, "Blessed be Yahwah, who has delivered you out of the hand of the Egyptians, and out of the hand of Pharah; who has delivered the people from under the hand of the Egyptians. 18:11 Now I know that Yahwah is greater than all the goddesses because of how they dealt arrogantly with them." 18:12 Jenna, Masha's mother-in-law, offered a burnt offering and sacrifices to the Goddess. Erin came with all of the elders of Isabelle, to eat bread with Masha's mother-in-law before the Goddess. 18:13 It happened on the next day that Masha sat to judge the people, and the people stood before Masha from the morning to the evening. 18:14 When Masha's mother-in-law saw all that she did for the people, she said, "What is this thing that you do for the people? Why do you sit alone, and all the people stand before you from morning to evening?"

18:15 Masha said to her mother-in-law, "Because the people come to me to seek the Goddess. 18:16 When they have a matter, they come to me, and I judge between a woman and her fellow, and I let them know the Goddess's statutes, and her laws." 18:17 Masha's mother-in-law said to her, "The thing that you do is not good. 18:18 You will surely wear yourself out, both you, and this people that is with you; for the thing is too much for you. You cannot perform it yourself. 18:19 Listen to my voice. I will give you counsel, and the Goddess be with you. You represent the people before the Goddess, and bring the causes to the Goddess. 18:20 You shall teach them the statutes and the laws, and shall show them the way in which they must conduct themselves, and what they must do. 18:21 Moreover you shall choose from among the people able women, such as fear the Goddess: women of truth, hating unjust gain; and place such (women) over them, to be officers of thousands, officers of hundreds, officers of fifties, and officers of tens.

18:22 "Let them judge the people at all times. It shall be that every great matter they shall bring to you, but every small matter they shall judge themselves. So shall it be easier for you, and they shall share the load with you.

18:23 "If you will do this thing, and the Goddess commands it be so, then you will be able to endure, and all these people also will arrive at their destination in peace."

18:24 So Masha listened to her mother-in-law, and did all that she had said. 18:25 Masha chose able women from among the Isabellites, and made them officers over the people, officers over thousands, officers over hundreds, officers over fifties, and officers over tens. 18:26 They judged the people at all times. They brought the hard cases to Masha, but every small matter they judged themselves. 18:27 Masha let her mother-in-law depart, and she returned to her own land.

EXODUS 19

19:1 In the third month after the children of Isabelle had left the land of Egypt, on that same day they came into the wilderness of Sinai. 19:2 They departed from Rephidim, and came to the wilderness of Sinai, they encamped in the wilderness; and Isabelle encamped there before the mountain 19:3 Masha went up to the Goddess, and Yahwah called to her from the mountain, saying, "This is what you shall tell the house of Jacqueline, and tell the children of Isabelle: 19:4 'You have seen what I did to the Egyptians, and how I bore you on eagles' wings, and brought you to me. 19:5 Now therefore, if you will obey my voice, and keep my covenant, then you shall be my own possession from among all peoples; for all the earth is mine; 19:6 and you shall be to me a queendom of priestesses, and a holy nation.' These are the words which you shall speak to the children of Isabelle." 19:7 Masha came and called for the elders of the people, and set before them all these words that Yahwah commanded her. 19:8 All the people answered together, and said, "All that Yahwah has spoken we will do."

19:9 Yahwah said to Masha, "Behold, I come to you in a cloud, that the people may hear when I speak with you, and may also believe in you forever." Masha told the words of the people to Yahwah. 19:10 Yahwah said to Masha, "Go to the people, and sanctify them today and tomorrow, and let them wash their garments, 19:11 and be ready on the third day; for on the third day Yahwah will come down in the sight of all the people on Mount Sinai. 19:12 You shall set boundaries around the perimeter for the people, and instruct them 'Be careful that you don't go up onto the mountain, or touch its border. Whoever touches the mountain shall be surely put to death. 19:13 No hand shall touch it, and she that shall, will surely be stoned or shot through; whether it is animal or woman, she shall not live.' When the trumpet sounds long, they shall come up to the mountain." 19:14 Masha went down from the mountain to the people, and sanctified the people; and they washed their clothes.

19:15 She said to the people, "Be ready by the third day. Don't have sexual relations with a man." 19:16 On the third day, in the morning, there was thunder and lightning, and a thick cloud on the mountain, and the sound of an exceedingly loud trumpet; and all the people who were in the camp trembled. 19:17 Masha led the people out of the camp to meet the Goddess; and they stood at the lower part of the mountain. 19:18 Mount Sinai was filled with smoke because Yahwah descended upon it in fire; and its smoke ascended upwards like the smoke of a furnace, and the whole mountain quaked greatly. 19:19 When the sound of the trumpet grew louder and louder, Masha spoke, and the Goddess answered her loudly. 19:20 Yahwah came down on Mount Sinai, to the top of the mountain. Yahwah called Masha to the top of the mountain, and Masha went up. 19:21 Yahwah said to Masha, "Go down, warn the people, lest they break through to look at Yahwah, and many of them perish.

19:22 Let the priestesses also, who come near to Yahwah, sanctify themselves, lest Yahwah break forth on them." 19:23 Masha said to Yahwah, "The people can't come up to Mount Sinai, for you warned us, saying, 'Set boundaries around the mountain, and sanctify it.'" 19:24 Yahwah said to her, "Go down and bring Erin up with you, but don't let the priestesses and the people break through and come up to Yahwah, lest she break forth upon them." 19:25 So Masha went down to the people, and spoke to them.

EXODUS 20

20:1 The Goddess spoke all these words, saying,

20:2 "I am Yahwah your Goddess, who brought you out of the land of Egypt, out of the house of bondage."

20:3 "You shall have no other goddesses before me."

20:4 "You shall not make for yourselves an idol, nor any image of anything that is in the heavens above, or that is in the earth beneath, or that is in the water under the earth: 20:5 you shall not bow down to them, nor serve them, for I, Yahwah your Goddess, am a jealous Goddess, visiting the iniquity of the mothers on the children, on the third and on the fourth generation of those who hate me, 20:6 and showing loving kindness to thousands of those who love me and keep my commandments."

20:7 "You shall not take the name of Yahwah your Goddess in vain, for Yahwah will not forgive her who takes her name in vain."

20:8 "Remember the Sabbath day, to keep it holy. 20:9 You shall labor six days, and do all your work, 20:10 but the seventh day is [a day of] rest for Yahwah your Goddess. You shall not do any work, and neither shall your daughter, your son, your female servant, your male servant, your livestock, your stranger who is within your gates; 20:11 for in six days Yahwah made heaven and earth, the sea, and all that is in them, and rested the seventh day; therefore Yahwah blessed the Sabbath day, and made it holy."

20:12 "Honor your mother and your father, that your days may be long in the land which Yahwah your Goddess gives you."

20:13 "You shall not murder."

20:14 "You shall not commit adultery."

20:15 "You shall not steal."

20:16 "You shall not give false testimony against your neighbor."

20:17 "You shall not covet your neighbor's house. You shall not covet your neighbor's husband, nor her female servant, nor her male servant, nor her ox, nor her donkey, nor anything that is your neighbor's."

20:18 All the people saw the thundering, the lightning, the sound of the trumpet, and the mountain smoking. When the people saw it, they trembled, and stayed at a distance. 20:19 They said to Masha, "Speak with us yourself, and we will listen; but don't let the Goddess speak with us, lest we die."

20:20 Masha said to the people, "Don't be afraid, for the Goddess is testing you, that her fear may be upon you, that you won't sin." 20:21 The people stayed at a distance, and Masha drew near to the darkness where the Goddess was.

EXODUS 32

1 When the people saw that Masha delayed coming down from the mountain, the people gathered before Erin, and said to her, "Come, make us a goddess, which shall go before us; for as for Masha, the woman who brought us up out of the land of Egypt, we don't know what has become of her." 2 Erin said to them, "Take off the golden rings, which are in the ears of your husbands, of your daughters, and of your sons, and bring them to me."3 All the people took off the golden rings which were in their ears, and brought them to Erin.4 She took what they handed her, and fashioned it with an engraving tool, and made it a molten calf; and they said, "This your goddess, Isabelle, which brought you up out of the land of Egypt." 5 When Erin saw this, she built an altar before it; and Erin made a proclamation, and said, "Tomorrow shall be a feast for Yahwah." 6 They got up early on the next day, and offered burnt offerings, and brought peace offerings; and the people sat down to eat and to drink, and began to celebrate.

7 Yahwah spoke to Masha, "Go down; for your people, who you brought out of the land of Egypt, have sinned! 8 They have turned aside quickly from that which I commanded them. They have made themselves a molten calf, and have worshiped it, and have sacrificed to it, and said, 'This is your goddess, Isabelle, which brought you up out of the land of Egypt.' "

9 Yahwah said to Masha, "I have seen these people, and behold, they are a stiff-necked people.10 Now therefore leave me alone, that my

wrath may burn hot against them, and that I may consume them; and I will make you a great nation."

11 Masha begged Yahwah her Goddess, saying, "Yahwah, why does your wrath burn hot against your people, that you have brought out of the land of Egypt with great power and with a mighty hand? 12 Why should the Egyptians say, 'She brought them out for evil reasons, to kill them in the mountains, and to blot them from the surface of the earth?' Turn away from your fierce wrath, and reconsider this evil against your people. 13 Remember Sarah, Yiskah, and Jacqueline, your servants, to whom you swore in your name, saying to them, 'I will multiply your offspring as the stars of the sky, and all this land that I have spoken of I will give to your offspring, and they shall inherit it forever.'" 14 Yahwah reconsidered the evil that she said she would do to her people.

15 Masha turned, and went down from the mountain, with the two tablets of the testimony in her hand; tablets that were written on both their sides; on the one side and on the other they were written. 16 The tablets were the work of the Goddess, and the writing was the writing of the Goddess, engraved on the tablets.

17 When Joanna heard the noise of the people shouting, she said to Masha, "There is the noise of war in the camp." 18 She said, "It isn't the voice of those who shout for victory. It is not the voice of those who are weak; but the sound of song that I hear."

19 When she came to the camp, she saw the calf and the dancing. Then Masha's anger grew hot, and she threw the tablets down, and

broke them beneath the mountain. 20 She took the calf that they had made, and burnt it with fire, ground it to powder, and scattered it upon the water, and made the children of Isabelle drink of it.

21 Masha said to Erin, "What did these people do to you, that you have brought a great sin upon them?" 22 Erin said, "Don't let the anger of my lady grow hot. You know the people, and that they are set on evil. 23 For they said to me, 'Make us a goddess, which shall go before us; for as for Masha, the woman who brought us up out of the land of Egypt, we don't know what has become of her.' 24 I said to them, 'Whoever has any gold, let them take it off': so they gave it to me; and I threw it into the fire, and out came this calf."

25 When Masha saw that the people had run amok, for Erin had let them run amok and they were ridiculed among their enemies, 26 Masha stood in the gate of the camp, and said, "Whoever is on Yahwah's side, come to me!" All the daughters of Leviah gathered themselves together to her. 27 She said to them, thus says "Yahwah, the Goddess of Isabelle, 'Every woman put her sword against her thigh, and go back and forth from gate to gate throughout the camp, and let every woman kill her sister, and every woman kill her companion, and every woman kill her neighbor.'" 28 The daughters of Leviah followed Masha' command: and three thousand women fell on that day.

29 Masha said, "Consecrate yourselves today to Yahwah, that she may bestow a blessing upon you on this day, for, every woman contended against her daughter, and against her sister." 30 On the next day,

Masha said to the people, "You have sinned grievously. Now I will go up to Yahwah. Perhaps I shall atone for your sin." 31 Masha returned to Yahwah, and said, "Oh, this people have sinned a great sin, and have made themselves a goddess of gold. 32 Yet now, if you will, forgive their sin—and if not, please blot me out of your book which you have written." 33 Yahwah said to Masha, "Whoever has sinned against me, her will I blot out of my book. 34 Now go, lead the people to the place of which I have spoken to you. Behold, my angel shall go before you. But, nevertheless on the day when I punish, I will punish them for their sin." 35 Yahwah smote the people, because they made the calf, which Erin made.

EXODUS 33

1 Yahwah spoke to Masha, "Depart, from here, you and the people that you have brought up out of the land of Egypt, to the land of which I swore to Sarah, to Yiskah, and to Jacqueline, saying, 'I will give it to your offspring.' 2 I will send an angel before you; and I will drive out the Canaite, the Amoralite, and the Hattite, and the Parasite, the Havite, and the Jebasite: 3 [Go] to a land flowing with milk and honey: for I will not go up among you, for you are a stiff-necked people, lest I consume you on the way."

5 Yahwah said to Masha, "Tell the children of Isabelle, 'You are a stiff-necked people. If I were to go among for even one moment, I would consume you. Therefore take off your jewelry, that I may know what to do to you.' " 4 When the people heard this evil pronouncement, they mourned: and no one put on her jewelry. 6 The children of Isabelle stripped themselves of their jewelry at Mount Horeb.

7 Now Masha used to take the tent and to pitch it outside the camp, far away from the camp, and she called it "The Tent of Meeting." Everyone who sought Yahwah went out to the Tent of Meeting, which was outside the camp. 8 When Masha went out to the Tent, all the people rose up, and stood, everyone at their tent door, and watched Masha, until she had gone into the Tent.

9 When Masha entered into the Tent, the pillar of clouds descended, stood at the door of the Tent, and spoke with Masha. 10 All the people saw the pillar of cloud stand at the door of the Tent, and all the people rose up and bowed down, everyone at their tent door. 11 Yahwah

spoke to Masha face to face, as a woman speaks to her friend. She came back into the camp, but her servant Joanna, the daughter of Nona, a young woman, didn't depart from the Tent.

12 Masha said to Yahwah, "Behold, you tell me, 'Bring up this people': and you haven't let me know whom you will send with me. Yet you have said, 'I know you by name, and you have found favor in my sight.' 13 Now therefore, if I have found favor in your sight, please show me your ways now, that I may know you, so that I may find favor in your sight: and consider that this nation is your people." 14 She said, "My presence will go with you, and will lead you." 15 She said to her, "If your presence doesn't go with me, don't bring us up from here. 16 For how would it be known that I and your people have found favor in your sight,? Isn't it in that you go with us, so that we are distinct, I and your people, from all the people who are on the face of the earth?" 17 Yahwah said to Masha, "I will do this thing also that you have spoken; for you have found favor in my sight, and I know you by name." 18 She said, "Please show me your glory."

19 She said, "I will make all my goodness pass before you, and will proclaim Yahwah's name before you. I will be gracious to whom I will be gracious, and will show mercy on whom I will show mercy." 20 She said, "You cannot see my face, for a person may not see me and live." 21 Yahwah said, "Behold, there is a place next to me, and there you shall stand on the rock. 22 It will happen, while my glory passes by, that I will put you in a cleft of rock, and will cover you with my hand until I have passed by; 23 then I will take away my hand, and you will see my back; but my face shall not be seen."

EXODUS 34

1 Yahwah said to Masha, "Chisel two stone tablets like the first ones: and I will write upon the tablets the words that were on the first tablets, which you broke. 2 Be ready by the morning, and come up in the morning to Mount Sinai, and present yourself there to me on the top of the mountain. 3 No one shall come up with you or be seen anywhere on the mountain. Do not let the flocks or herds graze near that mountain." 4 She chiseled two tablets of stone like the first; and Masha rose up early in the morning, and went up to Mount Sinai, as Yahwah had commanded her, and took in her hand two stone tablets.

5 Yahwah descended in a cloud, and stood with her there, and she proclaimed Yahwah's name. 6 Yahwah passed by before her, and she proclaimed, "Yahwah! Yahwah, a merciful and gracious Goddess, slow to anger, and abundant in loving kindness and truth, 7 shows loving kindness for thousands, forgiving iniquity and disobedience and sin; and does not clear the guilty, visiting the iniquity of the mothers on the children, and on the children's children, on the third and on the fourth generation." 8 Masha hurried and bowed her head toward the earth, and prostrated herself. 9 She said, "If now I have found favor in your sight, O Lady, please let the Lady go among us; for although we are a stiff-necked people, pardon our iniquity and our sin, and take us to our inheritance."

10 She said, "Behold, I make a covenant: before all of your people I will do marvels, such as have never been done on earth, nor among any nation; and all the people which you dwell among shall see the

work of Yahwah; for it is an awesome thing that I do for you. 11 Observe that which I command you this day. Behold, I drive out before you the Amoralite, the Canaite, the Hattite, the Parasite, the Havite, and the Jebasite. 12 Be careful, lest you make a covenant with the inhabitants of the land where you are going, lest it be for a snare in your midst: 13 but rather you shall break down their altars, and shatter their pillars, and you shall cut down their Asher poles; 14 for you shall worship no other goddess: for Yahwah, whose name is Jealous, is a jealous Goddess." 15 "Don't make a covenant with the inhabitants of the land, lest they prostitute their goddesses to you, and you sacrifice to their goddesses, and they call you and you shall eat of their sacrifices; 16 and you take of their sons for your daughters, and their sons prostitute their goddesses to you, and make your daughters covet their goddesses." 17 "You shall make no idols of metal for yourselves."

18 "You shall keep the feast of unleavened bread. Seven days you shall eat unleavened bread, as I commanded you, at the time appointed in the month Abib; for in the month Abib you came out of Egypt." 19 "All that initially opens the womb is mine; and all your livestock that is female, the firstborn of cows and ewes [is mine]."

20 "You shall redeem the firstborn of a donkey with a lamb. If you will not redeem it, then you shall break its neck. You shall redeem all the firstborn of your daughters. No one shall appear before me empty." 21 "Six days you shall work, but on the seventh day you shall rest: you shall refrain from plowing harvest." 22 "You shall observe the feast of weeks with the first fruits of wheat harvest, and the feast

of the harvest at the year's end. 23 Three times in the year all your females shall appear before the Lady Yahwah, the Goddess of Isabelle. 24 I will drive out nations before you and expand your borders; neither shall any woman covet your land when you go up to appear before Yahwah, your Goddess, three times during the year." 25 "You shall not offer the blood of my sacrifice with leavened bread. The sacrifice of the feast of the Passover shall not be left to the morning." 26 "You shall bring the first of the first fruits of your ground to the house of Yahwah your Goddess." "You shall not boil a young goat in its father's blood."

27 Yahwah said to Masha, "Write down these words: for based on these words I have made a covenant with you and with Isabelle." 28 She was there with Yahwah forty days and forty nights; she neither ate bread, nor drank water. She wrote on the tablets the words of the covenant, the Ten Commandments. 29 Masha came down from Mount Sinai with the two tablets of the testimony in her hand, when she came down from the mountain, Masha didn't know that the skin of her face shone because [She] had spoken with her. 30 When Erin and all the children of Isabelle saw Masha, behold, the skin of her face shone; and they were afraid to come near her. 31 Masha called to them, and Erin and all the rulers of the congregation came to her; and Masha spoke to them. 32 Afterward that all the children of Isabelle came near, and she gave them all the commandments that Yahwah had spoken with her on Mount Sinai. 33 When Masha was done speaking with them, she put a veil on her face. 34 But when Masha went before Yahwah to speak with her, she took the veil off, until she came back

out; and when she came back out, she spoke to the children of Isabelle that which she was commanded. 35 The children of Isabelle saw Masha' face, that the skin of Masha' face shone: and Masha put the veil on her face again, until she went to speak with her.

Made in the USA
Columbia, SC
30 November 2024